JAN ... laimed
authors of books for young people. She has

... il as the Guardian
Award, the Observer Teenage Fiction Prize
and the Angel Award for Fiction. Her many
titles include *The Ennead*, *Frankie's Hat*,
At the Sign of the Dog and Rocket, *Feet and
Other Stories*, *Enough is too Much Already*,
The Hillingdon Fox and *A Can of Worms*.
Jan Mark lives in Oxford.

Books by the same author

Aquarius
A Can of Worms
Divide and Rule
The Ennead
Enough is too Much Already
Feet and Other Stories
The Hillingdon Fox

For younger readers

The Dead Letter Box
Dream House
Handles
Nothing to be Afraid of
Thunder and Lightnings
Trouble Half-way

Illustrated titles

Fun
Fur
Strat and Chatto
The Snow Maze
The Twig Thing

Great Frog and Mighty Moose

Jan Mark

Walker Books, London

For Mick Gowar

First published 1992 by Walker Books Ltd
87 Vauxhall Walk, London SE11 5HJ

© 1992 Jan Mark

The right of Jan Mark to be identified as author
of this work has been asserted by her in accordance
with the Copyright, Designs and Patents Act 1988.

Printed and bound in Great Britain by
Richard Clay Ltd, Bungay, Suffolk

British Library Cataloguing in Publication Data
A catalogue record of this book
is available from the British Library.

ISBN 0-7445-2155-6

Acknowledgements

Every effort has been made to trace the ownership of all copyrighted
material and to secure the necessary permission to reprint these selections.
In the event of any question arising as to the use of any material, the
publisher, while expressing regret for any inadvertent error, will be happy
to make the necessary correction in future printings.

Grateful acknowledgement is made to the following for permission to reprint the copyrighted material listed below:

Waterloo Music Co. Ltd for "Land of the Silver Birch", collected by Merrick Jarrett in FOLK SONGS OF CANADA.

Oxford University Press, Canada, for excerpt from "What Is a Canadian?" from Miriam Waddington's COLLECTED POEMS. Copyright © 1986 by Miriam Waddington. Reprinted by permission of Oxford University Press, Canada.

Faber and Faber Ltd for "Phyllidula" from COLLECTED SHORTER POEMS by Ezra Pound, published by Faber and Faber Ltd. Reprinted by permission of Faber and Faber Ltd.

Doubleday and Co. Inc. for "Trees" from JOYCE KILMER: POEMS, ESSAYS AND LETTERS, edited by Robert Cortes Holliday, published by Doubleday and Co. Inc., 1918.

André Deutsch Ltd for "Song of the Open Road" from I WOULDN'T HAVE MISSED IT by Ogden Nash, published by André Deutsch Ltd, 1983. Reprinted by permission of André Deutsch Ltd. (UK only)

Curtis Brown Ltd for "Song of the Open Road" from HAPPY DAYS by Ogden Nash. Copyright © 1932 by Ogden Nash. Reprinted by permission of Curtis Brown Ltd. (World excl USA & Canada)

Little, Brown and Company for "Song of the Open Road" (Candy is Dandy) from VERSES FROM 1929 ON by Ogden Nash. Copyright © 1930, 1932 by Ogden Nash. First appeared in the *New Yorker*. By permission of Little, Brown and Company. (USA & Canada)

Warner/Chappell Music Inc., USA, for "Big Yellow Taxi" (Joni Mitchell). Copyright © 1970 by Siquomb Publishing Corporation. All rights reserved. Used By Permission. (World excl UK & Eire)

Warner Chappell Music Ltd, London, for "Big Yellow Taxi" (Joni Mitchell). Reproduced by permission of Warner Chappell Music Ltd. (UK & Eire)

M. William Krasilovsky for "The Shooting of Dan McGrew", "The Ballad of Blasphemous Bill" and "The Cremation of Sam McGee". Copyright © 1909 Dodd Meade & Co. Used by permission of the estate of Robert Service c/o M. William Krasilovsky, 51 E. 42nd Street, Suite 1601, New York, New York 10017.

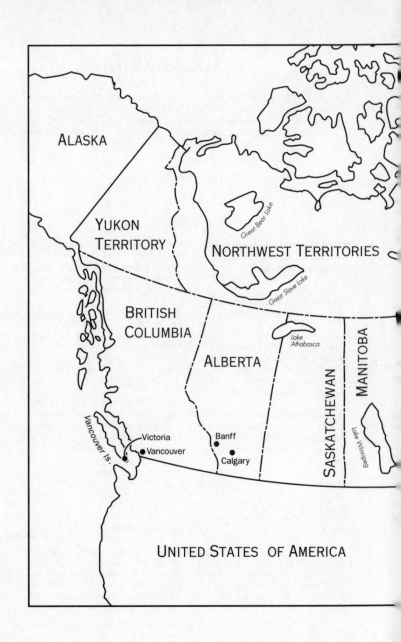

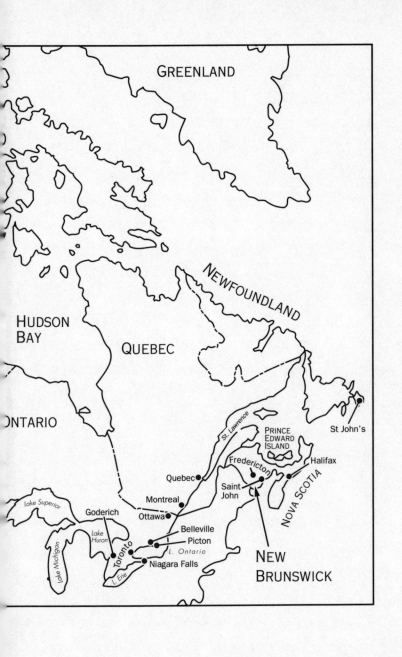

Chapter One

When we were at school we used to sing a song about Canada. It had a plaintive tune in a minor key:

Land of the silver birch, home of the beaver,
Where still the mighty moose wanders at will,
Blue lake and rocky shore, I will return once
      more,
Boom-tiddy-a-da boom-tiddy-a-da boom-
      tiddy-a-da
Boom.

I think the boom-tiddy-a-da bit was meant to represent the relentless throb of Indian drums, for half of us had to go on singing it while the other half progressed to the next verse, which mentioned wigwams.

Silver birches, mighty moose; my other image of Canada came from a jigsaw puzzle called "Luck for Two", which featured a couple of fishermen in a birch-bark canoe, landing a salmon. Behind them the sunset spread an orange glow across the sky, the water, their tartan shirts, and threw into relief the brooding silhouettes of the forest, not silver birch but Douglas fir.

Land of the Douglas fir, home of the salmon...

One day a breathless whisper went round the class at lunch-time: "There's a Canadian on the landing." One by one we crept out of the room to see him.

There was indeed a Canadian on the landing. I don't know quite what we were expecting, but if he'd come from another galaxy we could not have been more enthralled. He was very tall, his hair was longer than the current British fashion and his voice was incredibly deep, apparently emanating from somewhere around his hips, and he was so kind. I don't suppose it occurred to him for one instant why a dozen gawping ten-year-olds were clustering round him, but he talked to us just as if we were real people, which was not something that adults went in for much in those days.

We never found out why he was there. He chatted to us for about ten minutes, until the bell went, and we never saw him again. It wasn't an official visit ("Look, children, here is a real live foreigner"), he was someone who had called to see the head teacher and happened to be Canadian. This was just after the coronation of Queen Elizabeth. A few years later a photograph was published of her standing among her Commonwealth prime ministers. The prime minister of Canada, John Diefenbaker, was twice the size of any of the others, with a huge beaming smile and shoulders as wide as his own country. Another thought had lodged at the back of my mind: Canadians are very large.

Then there were the Mounties. We all knew about them, the North West Mounted Police. They wore red coats, Boy Scout hats, rode horses and always got their man. They also sang a song in French about pulling the feathers off skylarks.

In fact the whole country was viewed through the same fog of disinformation as any other nation at that time. The Dutch wore clogs and lived in windmills, the French wore little black berets and sold onions, while the Irish skipped about crying "Begorra!" and dug up leprechauns at the foot of the rainbow. Canada was no exception, but through it all persisted the memory of our Canadian on the landing at school; a happy memory. When at last, five years ago, I was invited to visit Canada I knew that secretly, and for ever, I had wanted to go there.

I was more clued up by this time. I knew, for instance, that the chances of meeting a mighty moose wandering at will through downtown Toronto were remote. I had a feeling that the Mounties would turn out to be cops in cars. I *knew* about Niagara Falls, separatism, maple syrup, seal hunting in New-foundland, grain production and the St Lawrence Seaway. Two of my favourite authors were Canadian. I even knew a short rude poem about a Canadian prime minister. In other words, I still knew practically nothing.

On the first visit I discovered that Canada is not so much the land of the silver birch as the land of the indoor tree. A Canadian house plant can be forty feet high. On the second visit I saw Niagara Falls and learned that this Marvel of Nature not only runs a hydro-electric power station but gets turned down at night. And by then I had realized that this enormous country was impossible to know. On the other hand,

I thought I ought to make the effort to get to know *something*, because it seemed impertinent to like it so much without understanding it, so I set off to cross it, from one side to the other. I didn't go north. My friend Janet said to me, "You will never understand Canada or Canadians unless you realize that the Arctic is part of us. An awareness of its being there – not of owning it, but a feeling that this otherness is ours."

This was why I didn't go north. I had three weeks in which to get across (it takes about six hours in an aeroplane) and clearly the Northern Territories are not somewhere you can drop in on. What I wanted to do was take a closer look at what I had seen already and to discover what I had overlooked before: the Maritime provinces – well, *one* Maritime province – French Canada, Vancouver Island and Bird House City, Ontario. There was also the small matter of the Canadian frog.

Never mind the mighty moose, the Mounties, the beaver. The beaver has been officially adopted as the emblem of Canada, but I hadn't travelled very far before I began to suspect that the creature that lies closest to the Canadian heart is the frog. It took me a long time to find out why. It isn't an obvious choice for a national symbol, which is no doubt why they settled for the beaver. Nevertheless, everywhere I went I was struck by a sense of frog, beginning, unforgettably, with the Great Frog of Fredericton, but that was only after I had started my journey proper, on the Atlantic Coast of Nova Scotia.

First of all, I had to visit a cemetery.

* * *

The young black man behind the counter was lean, quick and immaculate in his sharp white shirt and sober tie. He spoke urgently into a cordless phone.

"Can you send me two guys to section twenty-four ... the Littleton interment ... yeah, right away..."

What was going on? A riot? Outbreaks of fighting between rival mourners? An ambush at the graveside? I half expected the two guys to leap out of a doorway in combat gear, flak helmets well down over their eyes.

It turned out that he was just being efficient; no doubt this rapid deployment of personnel was an everyday routine. The undertaker who had come to the counter to request reinforcements murmured his thanks and turned away. There was no sound of distant gunfire. The young man put down his telephone and turned his attention to us, no less efficient. My friend David, who had come along for the ride, asked him for a guide to the cemetery.

Until I saw the place I hadn't thought about needing a guide, but as we drove up to the gate I'd seen a notice board announcing cheerfully: THINGS TO SEE AND DO WHILE VISITING MOUNT PLEASANT, and realized that you must be dead indeed if you visit a Canadian cemetery solely in order to get buried, particularly if you are visiting the Mount Pleasant Cemetery and Arboretum in Toronto. The notice continued: "We hope all visitors will observe the proprieties in these sacred grounds. Visitors are welcome to drive along Mount Pleasant's beautiful avenues. Increasingly, many people choose to derive full benefit of this beautiful environment by walking, bicycling and jogging through the property."

The message was unmistakable: *enjoy*. I wondered what sort of a reception you'd get if you went for a bike ride round an English cemetery.

While our young man was fetching us a map of the arboretum and a list of its hundreds of trees, I picked up some leaflets from the counter top; brochures for the latest line in gravestones and memorial tablets, advice on planning one's burial or cremation well in advance and paying for it by instalments as a hedge against inflation; arranging for after-care in the form of watering, weeding, fertilizing and grass-cutting around the plot in later years. These were published by the Toronto Cemeteries Trust. "Toronto Trust Cemeteries," they boasted modestly, "are widely known as the most beautiful cemeteries in Canada." I might have thought that this was a curious thing to boast about had I not begun to understand that many Canadian cemeteries are actually public parks; being buried in them is just one of the amenities on offer and, of course, by electing to be buried in one and making sure that your plot is properly looked after, you truly become part of your park.

Whenever I asked to be directed to an interesting cemetery people could always recommend their favourite, the one where they took the children for a walk, or exercised the dog, or regularly picnicked on Sunday afternoons. Almost everyone I spoke to had happy childhood memories of picnics in the cemetery.

I used to lurk in cemeteries as a child, lured there by a kind of morbid fascination. There is nothing morbid about Mount Pleasant. It really is pleasant. We drove through it in the September sunshine, acres of green turf, shrubs, magnificent trees – and tombstones. You can read the history of a city on its gravestones, and these are an instant reminder that Canada is a land founded by immigrants, for the graves have, as immigrants will, grouped themselves according to nationality. There is an Italian quarter, a Portuguese quarter, a Chinese quarter, a Scottish three-quarters, although there is nothing exclusive about this. Chinese lie among Catholic Italians, Presbyterian Scots among Koreans.

The stones ranged from discreet tablets in the grass to monumental obelisks. Some were engraved, some were sculpted, some bore photographs of the occupants. It was while I was admiring these that I noticed something rather unsettling. A fair number belonged to people who weren't even dead.

Back in the office, reading the leaflets, I'd been struck by the economics of death in Toronto. Pay now, die later seemed to be the watchword; sound advice, given the crippling cost of a funeral if you haven't been saving for it. This was the thinking behind the instalment plan. Our young man's colleague had been on the telephone explaining to a client the rate for engraving a memorial in Chinese – "Ten dollars per character, ma'am." Evidently, the more you have done at once, the cheaper it works out. Many of the stones bore the name of the deceased, with dates of birth and death, and the name of the next occupant alongside, accompanied by date of birth and a blank space to record the happy event, when it should occur. This seemed reasonable but, when we began to look for them, it turned out that there were as many stones which showed only the date of birth. Neither party was underground yet.

Somehow this made the whole business seem very reassuring. I could imagine Mr and Mrs Sanchez or Grandma and Grandpa Chung driving out on a fine evening to admire their own gravestones – almost as satisfying as reading your own obituary. The final visit would be as routine as a hairdressing appointment. It was easy to envisage the scene back in the cemetery office. "Oh yes, Mr Sapperstein, a very wise choice, beautiful stone. Wear it in good health!"

The older part of the cemetery was more traditional. Everyone was dead, for a start, except for the joggers and cyclists and parties of school kids sent out to the arboretum to do a project on trees.

"Mackenzie King is buried here somewhere," David said as we passed groves of urns, galleries of plinths, and a whole avenue of mausoleums with neat Grecian pediments over the doors.

This was the prime minister that I knew the poem about:

William Lyon Mackenzie King
Sat in the middle and played with string;
And he loved his mother like anything –
William Lyon Mackenzie King.

This hardly does him justice, as he was one of the politicians most responsible for making Canada a separate nation, long before the old British Empire broke up after the Second World War; but more of him later.

We didn't find the King grave but, whatever it looks like, it can hardly compete with the Massey mausoleum. The Masseys were a great and influential family and many things are named after them (including the tractors they made). The mausoleum is three stories high with turrets, lancet windows, Norman arches, steps, balustrades and a statue of Hope with an anchor, perched on top.

The Massey Mausoleum – Toronto

At first sight I thought it must be at least the crematorium. It occupies a large traffic island and is surrounded by tablets in memory of lesser Masseys. Wisteria clings to it, tall trees shade it. I imagine that a fair amount of wildlife hangs out in it. Dracula would have loved it.

Not far away, on a smaller traffic island, we saw a stone gazebo sheltering a statue of what looked like an attenuated panda. We went over for a closer inspection. The gazebo was a dome supported on columns, all carved from Laurentian granite, a great favourite in graveyards right across the country. It is exactly the colour of corned beef. The statue was black and white – hence the resemblance to a panda – but it was a human figure, carved out of white limestone, cruelly eroded and blackened with soot. It was all of a piece with its plinth, also white limestone, on which all the writing had weathered away, but its history was easy to decipher.

Some respectful family, emigrating from the Old World, had taken with them not only their household possessions but also the family tombstone, erecting it here in Toronto under its shiny new dome of Laurentian granite. Before that it must have stood for decades under a wet, dirty, northern English sky, fouled by smoky English air, scoured by bitter, acid English rain. I could guess how happy the family must have felt about it, gathering round to admire it as it stands now, clean and cosy under its new Canadian lid, a permanent reminder of the British grot they had left behind.

Chapter Two

At Pearson Airport next morning I got into conversation with a lady who was trekking across country to get home for a funeral in St John's, Newfoundland. It had been a hairy trip so far. Her husband had driven her 805 kilometres through the night to catch the flight to Toronto.

"It was terrifying," she said, "there were all these moose in the road."

Thinking of hedgehogs in England I envisioned whole stretches of the Trans-Canada Highway littered with flattened moose. That's what comes of wandering at will, I thought, but she explained that they just stand around in the road, getting seriously in the way. Given that a moose is about the size of a cart horse, they must be a considerable traffic hazard, especially after dark.

Now she was heading for Halifax, on the penultimate leg of her journey, and so was I, although it was the first leg of mine.

Halifax, capital of Nova Scotia: once it was called Chebucto; it narrowly escaped being called Dunk. The original inhabitants were Meeg-a-maage Indians.

The British, as usual refusing to get their tongues round anyone else's language, called them Mick-amucks to begin with, and finally Micmacs. The Micmacs, who are still around, called the place, very accurately, Che-book-took, "at the biggest harbour". The first white settlers managed to turn that into Chebucto. These were the French, who had their own name for the region. They called it Acadie, either because they wanted to name it after the Ancient Greek heaven-on-earth, Arcadia, or because they had, like everyone else, mistaken the Micmac word *a-ka-de* (place of) for the name of the place. Either way it remained Acadie until the British barged in and in 1755 began deporting the French settlers who were doing no harm at all, except by living where the British wanted to live. Many of them went south, to Louisiana, where the name changed again, and the people who said that they were Acadians became know as Cajuns.

In 1749 the English had begun to build a new town "at the biggest harbour" and named it after George Dunk, who organized the settlement. His title was Earl of Halifax which, admittedly, has a finer ring to it than Dunk.

Nova Scotia, like a lobster on a string, hangs out into the Atlantic, and would be an island if it were not for the Chignecto Isthmus that holds it on to the mainland of Canada. Built on that biggest harbour, now called the Bedford Basin, Halifax looks much more like a European city than I had expected. No North American city really looks European, whatever the locals may think; none of them has been there long enough to have acquired that European air of imminent collapse – except perhaps New York – but Halifax does not immediately look Canadian either and I'd decided that even from the aeroplane. It is without skyscrapers. It has tall buildings, but remembering previous descents into Canadian capitals, I'd been looking out for the downtown core, the unmistakable frieze of rectangles, the Lego centre. There wasn't one. Better still, there was no tower.

One of my last sights of Toronto, as we took off, had been the CN Tower. It is the world's tallest free-standing structure, a transmitter with, inevitably, a revolving restaurant on top. One can ascend to an observation platform by lift, a height of 361 metres. I haven't been up it. You get exactly the same view from an aircraft at 361 metres, which is one of the drawbacks to air travel. It has taken the excitement out of looking down from tall buildings. There are similar, though shorter, towers at Niagara Falls, Calgary and Vancouver. I haven't been up any of them.

As far as I can make out, everyone in Toronto laughs at the CN Tower, but they can't help drawing your attention to it – there are very few places in the city which do not have a view of the CN Tower. Secretly they are waiting for it to fall down. Canadians are the world's most gleeful pessimists. When I first visited Calgary, artificial ski jumps were being built for the Winter Olympics, and artificial snow machines installed. "It'll all blow away," said the Calgarians, hopefully. "The Chinook wind will melt it." The last time I was in Toronto a vast, all-weather sports stadium was under construction, with a sliding roof. "It will stick," said the Torontonians. "Open." In fact it is now finished and working perfectly, much to everyone's disappointment, no doubt.

But in Halifax, no tower; no skyscrapers. In the distance I could see the city spread out over hills and valleys around the Bedford Basin. There were bridges, ships; I saw three industrial smokestacks painted in red and white stripes, but the airport seemed to be surrounded by forest. It was a damp, grey, sunless day, an Atlantic day, which was right and proper. Halifax is an Atlantic port, a working port, a naval base. It isn't drab, or dirty, but it has a functional feel, an air of having its sleeves rolled up. There is a plush new shopping mall on Barrington Street and some shiny refurbishment of old warehouses on the waterfront, but there are no frills, no gloss. Halifax has something better to do with its time.

Norene met me at the airport.

"What would you like to see while you are in Halifax?" said Norene.

"Lead me," I said, "to your cemetery."

Norene did a double take. "That's what you want to see?"

"If you know of a good one."

Norene said that she would show me her favourite graveyard, and added that there was quite a choice specimen on Barrington, but what *else* would I like to see?

"Show me *your* favourite bits." I learned long ago that the best way to see a new city is to walk round it with someone who lives there and loves it. "There's the Citadel, of course," Norene said, "and the memorial to the Explosion ... and Julie's Pond."

"Who's Julie? What's with her pond?"

"Everyone goes there in spring to hear the frogs."

I wished it were spring. In fact it was autumn, or about to be. All good frogs were retiring for the winter, but my pulses quickened. Norene could not know it, but she had touched a chord. I have this thing about frogs. I write about them. I have to make an effort *not* to write about frogs. Some writers feel that way about rainbows, daffodils, beautiful women; with me it's frogs. I even managed to get frogs into a novel about motorcycles.

"Are the Maritimes a frogful place?" I asked, hesitantly.

"Well, there's a very large one in Fredericton, New Brunswick," Norene said.

"A large frog?" I tried to control myself. "A real one?"

"Stuffed," Noreen said.

Stuffed! I've seen mummified frogs. We once had a small collection of them in an ice-cream carton – the two-litre size – but I'd never come across a stuffed frog. "Tell me about it."

Maddeningly, there was not much to tell. It had not been an especially heroic or talented frog, but as somebody's pet it had grown very large and was stuffed as a keepsake. Now it is in a museum. Why not? Few people know that, back in England, there is a stuffed dog in a glass case on Platform One at the station in Slough, Berks.

Even more maddeningly, New Brunswick is right next door to Nova Scotia, on the other side of the Chignecto Isthmus, about two hundred and twenty-five kilometres away; a short hop in Canadian terms, but I hadn't allowed enough time for a visit.

The Great Frog of Fredericton haunted me all the way across Canada. Occasionally I met someone who had heard of it. On my very last night I met someone who had actually *seen* it, but people were tantalizingly vague. It assumed an almost mythic quality. One day I shall make a pilgrimage to Fredericton.

Norene consoled me by explaining that there was quite a large frog in the middle of Halifax, and promised to show it to me next morning.

I checked in at the hotel on Morris Street, named, I would guess, after the surveyor who mapped out the plans for the original settlement back in the eighteenth century. Then I took the map that Norene had given me and went walkabout on the waterfront. I went northward, past the wharves. Near the Museum Wharves I passed a children's adventure playground. Instead of the usual fortress or assault course, the construction inside was built like the skeleton of a ship. I wasn't sure at first if it really was an adventure playground, for on the fence was a notice: FOR YOUR SAFETY, STAY OFF THE SCULPTURE.

Could the ship be a sculpture? Surely not; it must have been designed for climbing on. No one could possibly put up something like that and then tell people not to climb on it. I looked round.

The sculpture was behind me, and so large that I wondered how I had missed it, a huge, smooth, grey slope of ... of... It was hard to make out quite what it was made of, or what it was meant to be. There was something of the whale about it, the sweep of a whale's great fluke as it sports in the ocean. Halifax was, for a time, a whaling port.

This was only a first impression. Closer to, it looked more like an enormous tongue, an impression reinforced by a small dent in the ground, immediately below the tip and apparently placed to catch the drips.

Now, there are plenty of places in the world that would cheerfully display a sculpture of a huge slavering tongue, but it seemed to me that Halifax is not one of them. I walked all round it, almost under it, for it curved high above my head. I couldn't see any identification, no name, not even the name of its sculptor, but it was surrounded by a substantial chain-link fence and affixed to the fence was another notice. It had a weary air about it, as if erected by people at their wits' end. The way it had been written out rather resembled a poem:

> This temporary fence
> has been erected as
> a public safety measure
> and will be removed when
> a permanent solution
> has been established.

It was signed by the Waterfront Corporation Ltd. I walked all round the sculpture again. What on earth had been going on? It was surely too steep to climb, not high enough to attract suicides, too large to trip over in the dark. When later I met Norene for supper, I asked her about it.

"Oh," said Norene, "that's The Wave."

I felt ashamed. Of course it was a wave, vast, curved, caught and petrified at the very moment of breaking. "But why is it fenced off?"

"Skateboarders," Norene said succinctly. Of course, again; that irresistible ogival slope from the trough to the crest, the lure of the last split-second twist as the board reached the summit of its ascent – not so much skateboarding as skate-surfing. I could only too well imagine what had been happening to the less skilful skaters who had failed to turn in time; hence the notice, put up by the Waterfront Corporation, exasperated at having to scrape yet another overshot skateboarder off the concrete.

I hadn't had much luck searching out Halifax's candidate for the Good Cemetery Guide. The Old Burying Ground on Barrington would have been perfect, only it was closed for renovations. The English have a short way with disused graveyards. The men from the council come along, yank the tombstones out of the ground, stack them neatly along one side and install park benches. The Old Burying Ground really was being renovated. Behind the locked gates men were busy with block and tackle, straightening old stones like orthodontists, rebuilding table tombs and, as far as I could see, having an enjoyable poke around at what lay beneath.

Next day, though, we drove out to see Norene's local cemetery, Fairview Lawn.

Norene said, "I'll show you the *Titanic* graves."

"*Titanic* graves?"

Like most people – outside of Halifax – I'd always assumed that those who were not rescued from the *Titanic* had drowned, going down with, or being sucked down by, the enormous liner as she went to the bottom of the Atlantic.

Graves of the Titanic victims – Halifax

Everyone knows the story: on Wednesday, 10 April 1912, the largest ship ever built set sail on her maiden voyage from Southampton, carrying 2,206 passengers and, with room aboard them for scarcely half that number of people, twenty lifeboats. Four days later, on the evening of the fourteenth, the *Titanic* struck an iceberg. It was shortly before midnight. Within hours the ship, designed to be unsinkable, had sunk. About seven hundred passengers and crew found room in the lifeboats; the rest were drowned, below decks or in the open water. That part is well known. Films have been made about the *Titanic*,

books written. In 1985 a midget submarine located
and photographed the broken hulk on the seabed. It
is still, eighty years later, thought of as an awful
warning, the punishment of hubris; its wreck is
designated a grave. But as far as most of us know, it
is the only grave. I had no idea that in the cemetery
of Fairview Lawn, above the Bedford Basin in
Halifax, Nova Scotia, lie the graves of 125 of the
victims whose bodies were taken from the water.
They rest below curving rows of low grey stones,
sober, unostentatious as the *Titanic* never was, as
though the people who erected the memorial
understood that to build something large and
imposing would be no less than a final insult to the
men, women and children who had died in that great
floating folly.

Some of the stones carry inscriptions, most bear
only the name and some, not even that. *Child* ...
woman...

On a few of the graves fresh flowers were lying.

I suppose that the loss of the *Titanic* could be
regarded as the first modern disaster. So many people
were involved. If it happened today it would still be
accounted a disaster, in spite of the horrors we see
daily on television. Halifax was only a sad witness to
the *Titanic*, and host to her dead, but within six years
an even greater catastrophe occurred, this time in the
city itself.

The Citadel, the great fortress that stands above
Halifax, never saw a shot fired in anger. The French
never came against it by land or sea, but the city was
a garrison, a naval base, and, in World War One, a

port of embarkation for men and munitions bound across the Atlantic to Europe.

On the morning of 6 December 1917, a French munitions ship, the *Mont Blanc*, was entering the Bedford Basin to join a convoy when she collided with a Belgian ship, the *Imo*. The collision was a minor one, but the *Mont Blanc* was carrying gun cotton, explosive picric acid and TNT and, on her deck, benzol in tins. The collision damaged the tins, the benzol ignited. The captain and crew abandoned ship, and fled to shore while the *Mont Blanc* drifted, burning. Ships in the dockyard sent boarding parties to help the city fire department fight the blaze. They were both approaching the *Mont Blanc* and aboard her when she exploded.

The writer Thomas Raddall, who saw it, describes the explosion as "a pillar of white smoke, reaching a mile into the sky and unfolding at the top in greasy grey convolutions like an incredible toadstool."

It reads like the description of a nuclear explosion, and in a smaller way the effects were much the same. A whole square mile of the city was flattened, the wooden houses catching fire. In Halifax and Dartmouth, across the Basin, sixteen hundred people died, and nine thousand were injured. Corpses and survivors were being dragged from the ruins days later. It was the depths of winter. Heavy snow fell.

Norene said that, even now, digging in the garden, you may come to a layer of ash.

Above the Basin, on a hilltop, stands the stark memorial to the victims of the explosion. Its bells still ring for the dead.

On the waterfront of Halifax is a museum. One corner of it has been rebuilt to represent what originally stood upon the site, a ships' chandlers, and beside it, in a dark passageway, there is a little white double tombstone. It stood there in December 1917, waiting to be collected by its owner, a man whose two small children had died. It was to be placed upon the grave they shared. When the *Mont Blanc* went up, at five past nine on the morning of 6 December, he and the rest of the family were wiped out. There was no one left to claim the stone, or erect it; no one left who knew *where* to erect it, and so, at last, it has been returned to stand where it stood before the explosion, a memorial to the whole family.

We were due back in the city for lunch. There was just time to drive out to Hemlock Ravine to see Julie's Pond, and here I learned the peculiar love story of Julie and Edward.

She was Alphonsine Thérèse Bernadine Julie de Montgenet de Saint Laurent.

He was Prince Edward.

He was a son of George III; she was a French Canadian, and they met while he was commanding the garrison at Quebec. It would not be quite true to say that he was the best of George's sons, but he was perhaps the least worst. They were not at all a respectable family.

In any case, Edward was pompous, extravagant to the point of lunacy and an enthusiastic hanger-and-flogger, but on the credit side he was intelligent enough to be a career soldier, and he loved his Julie.

I don't know if anyone has written a historical romance about these two, but if not I can't think why not. It's a wonderful plot. Because he was a royal prince and she was a commoner (and perhaps because he was a Protestant and she a Catholic – better and better) they could not marry. But they lived ecstatically together and when Edward was appointed to command the Halifax garrison in 1794, Julie came with him.

It was the time of the Napoleonic Wars, when Halifax waited for an armada to cross the Atlantic and recapture Canada for France. It may be that Julie would have been in favour of that, but, faithful to Edward, she stayed with him as he set about building in the heart of Halifax a citadel as mighty and impregnable as the one he had left behind in Quebec. For a time they lived in a house overlooking the barracks, but then the governor offered them his country house, out at Hemlock Ravine on the Bedford Basin. He must have been a romantic type himself, for the house is named after a place in *Romeo and Juliet*, Friar Laurence's Cell.

Edward, with a garrison of troops at his disposal, set them to landscaping the grounds, cutting out paths to form the letters of Julie's name, building a music pavilion and little summer houses with wind chimes hanging in the eaves. He had a pond constructed, in the shape of Julie's heart, which seems to have been singularly long and thin. A whole company of soldiers was stationed there to protect the couple and when the snow fell, and threatened to cut off Hemlock Ravine from the rest of Halifax, out came the troops to shovel it away. In between whiles Edward hanged and flogged them more or less as a matter of routine. When he finally left Canada in 1800, with several of his men under sentence of death for mutiny, he presented the city with a magnificent clock tower which stands there to this day, a reminder of how much of his troops' time he managed to waste.

It was duty that parted Edward and Julie. She ended her days in a Belgian convent, for Edward was forced, in the end, to do the decent thing – for a man in his position, the son of a king. He went home, married a German princess and had an heir.

The heir was a daughter, born in 1819, the year before her father died – it was a close run thing – and she lived to be Queen of England. Yes! Edward's daughter was Queen Victoria. What she would have made of all that frolicking out in the ravine we can only guess. She was a very moral woman, but also passionate and romantic. She would have liked the heart-shaped pond. It's the kind of thing that British royalty goes in for in a big way. It's still there, and in spring, as Norene said, Haligonians go out to Hemlock Ravine to listen to the frogs, who are also feeling pretty romantic at that time of year.

This particular kind of frog is extremely small and known as a "peeper", for the noise it makes and not, as I had at first supposed, from its habit of lurking in the bushes and spying on other frogs. The peeper is dear to the hearts of Haligonians. They are so fond of it that they have made an enormous model of a peeper and fixed it to the wall of the Nova Scotia Museum of Anthropology and Natural History.

"They take him in in the fall," Norene said, "but in spring he is put out again and by some device is made to 'peep' in season."

I was seriously alarmed in case the peeper had already been taken in to hibernate, but when we reached the Nova Scotia Museum of Anthropology and Natural History, there he was, several metres high and clinging to the wall, peering coyly round the corner. He wasn't the Great Frog of Fredericton, but he was some frog.

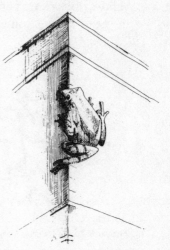

After lunch I walked down to the waterfront and took the ferry across the harbour to Dartmouth. The ferries are nice buoyant little boats, rounded at either end so that, from a distance, they appear

East Coast Frog.
'Peeper' Nova Scotia
Natural History Museum
– Halifax

to be almost spherical. Halifax settled down and stretched itself along the shore line as we drew out into the waterway and Dartmouth approached. The waterfront on this side was tree lined, with grassy stretches, waterside walks and benches where you could sit to enjoy the view.

As we came closer the trees near the ferry terminal took on an exotic appearance. Some were evergreen, some deciduous and nearly leafless, but they were all brilliant with yellow blossom. When the ferry docked I walked south, on the path above the shore, until I came to the trees. The yellow blossoms were not blossoms at all, they were ribbons, hundreds of yellow ribbons tied around branches and twigs; some in neat bows, some fluttering in lean streamers.

Tree with Yellow Ribbons – Halifax

Some were plain, others bore messages and names written in felt-tip. I remembered then that this is a naval port. Only a week or so earlier the Canadian Government had sent a fighter squadron and three warships to the Persian Gulf, to support the UN blockade after Iraq invaded Kuwait at the beginning of August. The planes had left from bases in Germany. From Halifax had sailed the three ships: two destroyers, HMS *Athabaskan* and HMS *Terra Nova*, and a supply ship, HMS *Protecteur*, carrying 934 sailors and between them having clocked up seventy years of service. As someone said at the time, "Canadians ... do not perceive themselves as a military people." But they were helping out, as usual. The ships had had to undergo a hurried refit in Halifax before heading out to what was certain to become a war zone. As someone else said at the time, "Those ships are *inviolable* unless the Iraqis attack them with paint thinner."

Things were much the same in the First World War. The entire Atlantic fleet, HMCS *Niobe*, was stationed at Halifax while the Pacific fleet, HMCS *Rainbow*, was on the other side of the country, lying off Vancouver Island.

It is an American custom to tie yellow ribbons around trees as a homecoming token, but it has spread north across the border. On the shore at Dartmouth the ribbons snapped and rustled in the wind from the Atlantic.

To pass the time while waiting for the ferry back to the Halifax side, I bought myself something to read from the newsagent on the terminal. For daily news I'd been relying on the national paper, the *Globe and Mail*; now I thought I'd try some tabloids, especially as one of them promised, on the front page, a photograph of an angel. Beat that, *Sunday Sport*, I thought.

Most of the tabloids had also spread north across the border from the United States. Things were different down there. As well as the angel's mug shot the *Weekly World News* offered a man who had sent his wife back to the Stone Age in a time machine, a mermaid's skeleton found in a shark's stomach (artist's impression but no photo) and the startling information that Queen Elizabeth's favourite pastime is stripping down Rolls-Royce engines. Its rival, the

National Examiner, featured a corpse waking up after seventy-two years, an outbreak of vampires in Exeter, Rhode Island, another angel, who had plucked a plunging paratrooper from the sky, and a kitten in Seattle who was savaging neighbours and large dogs. ("*The mad mouser suddenly turned on her and RIPPED huge chunks of flesh from her hands...*") I also learned that Elvis Presley had miraculously appeared to US troops in Saudi dressed as Lawrence of Arabia.

Back on land I sat in a sheltered spot, wrote some postcards home and then went in search of the post office to mail them. I particularly wanted to send them from the post office because in post offices the mail boxes are built into the wall and cannot get away. For some reason, Canadian mail is kind of leisurely. This is odd because the Canadian mail box outnumbers the British pillar box quite heavily, but the mail boxes, which have legs, hang around on corners, sometimes singly, or in pairs, sometimes in conspiratorial groups. It occurred to me, some years ago, that I had never witnessed a Canadian mail box being emptied, and I'd begun to formulate the theory that when a mail van is seen approaching, the mail boxes, on their legs, shuffle round the corner and hightail it for the hills.

Then I walked back to the hotel, along Barrington, down Morris, pausing at the store on the corner to buy a submarine. I'd been wondering about submarines ever since I'd arrived in Halifax. Every other shop, it seemed, carried a sign offering submarines for sale. Fair enough, I'd thought, this is a naval base, but then I noticed that all the shops that sold submarines were groceries, cafés and supermarkets. It turned out that they are small baguette loaves, cut across and filled with salad, salami, cheese, ham, to make a submarine-shaped sandwich. One of these was about half the price of a British Rail sandwich and contained an entire meal. I bought mine for supper, with some apples and a carton of juice, and returned to the hotel to watch the speaking clock.

Halifax has the world's spookiest television station, and if I'd arrived only a week later I'd have missed it. The previous night, before going out to supper with Norene, I'd been idly flipping channels in my room to see what was on offer. In addition to its own services, Canada receives a tidal wave of transmissions from the US. Occasionally I managed to find a news bulletin. There was a local station which economically combined reading the news with selling second-hand cars. An unseen newscaster detailed the day's events while on the screen appeared slides of the cars with price and telephone number in subtitles.

After supper, still searching for some international news in the hope of catching up on the Gulf crisis, I discovered this eeriest channel of all, a public service station apparently devoted to telling the time. The screen was green, an invisible clock ticked remorse-lessly; the caption read:

PROCEEDINGS OF THE HOUSE OF COMMONS RESUME
MONDAY SEPTEMBER 24, 1990
13.00 E.T.
CBC
SATELLITE NETWORK

ET stood for Eastern Time, which was the crux of the whole enterprise. Canada has six time zones. Two voices took turns to read the time across the continent, in English and French.

"Co-ordinated Universal Time 0 hours 6 minutes exactly. Newfoundland Daylight Time 21 hours 51 minutes 40 seconds. Atlantic Daylight Time 21 hours 21 minutes 50 seconds. Eastern Daylight Time 20 hours 8 minutes 10 seconds. Central Daylight Time 19 hours 8 minutes 40 seconds. Mountain Daylight Time 18 hours 8 minutes 40 seconds. Pacific Daylight Time 17 hours 8 minutes 50 seconds..." It took three whole minutes to read the time right across Canada. We had come around to Universal Co-ordinated again and I thought they might stop, but no, on they went. We were on Atlantic Time in Halifax. Newfoundland is half an hour out of step. I left them to it and went out.

That evening I switched on eagerly and there they were again, Joe and Jacques, as I privately named them, still intoning their Anglo-French antiphon; Mountain Daylight Time ... Pacific Daylight Time ... Universal Co-ordinated...

At one in the morning, out of sheer curiosity, I tuned in once more. They were still at it.

Chapter Three

Next morning it poured with rain. Mindful of all the warnings I'd received about wild climatic changes, I was carting along with me a hefty load of sweaters, scarves and gloves that I thought I *might* need. Most of the time, though, the only essential items of equipment were sunglasses and an umbrella. Unfortunately I had left both in Toronto.

Never mind, I thought, contemplating the rain-washed tarmac at the airport; once we get above the clouds it will be a fine day. Above the clouds it's always a fine day, and today would be no exception.

Today was an exception. Sure, the sun was up there somewhere but we never saw it. When our flight was called, instead of embarking through the usual tunnel, warm and weatherproof, we were herded and driven along corridors, down stairs, out of a doorway – on to the tarmac. The rain hissed disagreeably. A hundred yards away stood a row of aircraft, most of them jets. Ours was straight ahead, a little de Havilland Dash, with four propellers. *Propellers.* I was chalking up another first; I had never before flown in a prop-driven aircraft.

Inside it was snug; about half the size of the Oxford-London coach with, like a coach, a long rear seat. There was one stewardess who brought round sweets and drinks and morning papers. The paper carried a banner headline: CANADA ON THE BRINK OF RECESSION. It felt like being at home.

Across the aisle from me two off-duty pilots eyed the headline with disfavour.

"Scaremongering," murmured one. "Now everyone'll think the plane's about to run out of fuel and drop out of the sky."

The plane, though, was climbing doggedly, through dirty cloud. Halifax was swallowed up almost before I had time to look out and say goodbye. I had feared the worst, juddering, lurching, yawing and, maybe, ditching, in such rotten weather, but it rose smoothly, engines humming. It was no noisier, no rougher, and certainly no less comfortable than a small jet; there was perhaps more of an air of effort about its climb, and we never did get above the clouds, but it was cosy inside the Dash and by the time we landed at Saint John, where half of the passengers got out, we were practically on first-name terms with the stewardess. The two jolly pilots also left at Saint John. The Dash, now much lighter, hopped into the sodden air again and headed for Quebec.

The view from the window continued to be various shades of grey. I was reminded of the worst flight I ever endured, through the fringes of a hurricane between Boston and New York, in a nasty aircraft called a Whisperliner which looked, and felt, as if it had been hurriedly cobbled together out of bits of other aeroplanes. There was no life raft under my seat and the overhead luggage bins sagged. The Dash, by comparison, felt reassuringly airworthy. Only one thing spoiled my enjoyment of the flight and that ruined it entirely. At the back of my mind a mean voice was muttering, "When you get to Quebec, you'll have to speak French."

The province of Quebec used to be called New France. It is three times bigger than old France and eighty per cent of the population speak French. Canada is part of the Commonwealth and the Queen of England (the motor mechanic, yes, *that* queen) is also Queen of Canada. It was not always so and it may not be so again. Before it was British, Canada was French. If Leif Eriksson, the Viking explorer, had hung on a bit longer, it might have been Scandinavian. And the United States has always had its eye on Canada.

The Italian explorer Cabot, sailing under an English flag, claimed the new found land (Newfoundland) for England, but the first man to go inland was a Frenchman, Jacques Cartier, who sailed up the St Lawrence River as far as the island where now stands the city of Montreal, and claimed the area for France. The locals, who were Iroquois Indians, used the word *kanata* for a village. Cartier, thinking that it referred to the whole area, used it too; Kanata; Canada.

It was Samuel de Champlain, the founder of Acadie, who first started a settlement at what became the city of Quebec in 1608. Catholic emigrants went out there from France to farm, but many disappeared into the interior of this great unmapped territory to make a fortune from freelance fur trapping. Some of them, travelling overland and by canoe, got as far as the Rockies. Two brothers-in-law, Pierre Radisson and Medart Chouart des Groseilliers, went north and discovered an enormous bay in the sea that lay beyond Lake Superior. It struck them immediately that in future, instead of shipping furs by canoe from Lake Superior to Montreal and then down the St Lawrence to the sea, it would be much more economical to send them direct from the bay and out into the Atlantic. The French were not interested. The English were. The Hudson's Bay Company was formed in 1670, a British presence in the north, thanks to the two Frenchmen – Radish and Gooseberry, as the English called them.

You might imagine that Canada, although then much smaller than it is now, was big enough to leave room for not only the French and the British to settle there, but anyone else who felt like joining in. But by now, back in Europe, England and France were at war, endlessly taking and retaking each other's lands in the New World as they skirmished in the Old. The beginning of the end came in 1759, when General Wolfe attacked the French troops of General Montcalm on the Plains of Abraham, above Quebec city. The French surrendered and a year later Montreal fell to a British fleet. Eventually, what had been New France was split into two: Upper Canada and Lower Canada. If you look at them on a map, Upper Canada is some way south of Lower Canada, but it was named for being further upstream. In Upper Canada they spoke English and they still do, for now it is the province of Ontario.

Lower Canada became the province of Quebec. And they still speak French.

I can speak French, and read it, but I don't understand it very well when spoken to me, and here I was heading for a city where French is the first language of most of the population, many of whom, I had been told frequently, fiercely resent having to speak English at all.

"You'll be all right," said my friend Kathy, in Toronto. "Most of them are bilingual. There are very few French who *refuse* to speak English." They are the ones I shall run into, I thought. Then, as an afterthought, she added, "Just make sure that they know you're English and not Anglo-Canadian."

She didn't enlarge upon what would happen if I were mistaken for an Anglo, but I didn't think it was a mistake anyone was likely to make. The British abroad have a look about them, not dirty exactly, but not quite fresh. This may be because we don't, on the whole, have special clothes to go abroad in, unless we are soccer hooligans going to Europe. Wearing my old black trench coat I was fairly certain that I would never be taken for any kind of Canadian – and certainly not for an American. While pounding the streets of Halifax, in the trench coat, I kept running across a party of old ladies from Florida, all with identical white and pastel golf shoes, identical white and pastel jogging tops, identical white and pastel hair styles, identical slacks in pink, blue, lemon or lime green. I came to recognize them from a distance, dithering across the street ahead of me at intersections, or silting up outside restaurants and theatres. In the end I realized what it was that they reminded me of – a pack of Tic-tacs – and when I saw the Tic-tacs converging I turned down a side street. It took so long to get *through* them.

But boy, were they clean.

My first attempt at speaking French in Quebec was undertaken in the worst conditions imaginable – over the phone, at the airport. I had to find somewhere to stay. I rang the tourist centre and asked about hotels.

Apparently there was nothing wrong with my accent or vocabulary, for the nice lady at the tourist centre answered rapidly. I think it was at this point that I finally began to understand that the Québécoises are not simply Canadians who don't like speaking English. They are people who speak French and happen to live in Canada. I had to stop my tourist lady fast, before it was my turn to answer; well, slow her down, anyway. I pleaded cravenly, "*Madame, s'il vous plait, lentement, plus lentement. Je suis Anglaise.*"

Oh, the shame. But the effect was instantaneous, and staggering. Francophone or not, she was as kind as any Canadian and switched to English, almost in mid-sentence, without a trace of a French accent. What I had been told by several people proved to be true, as I discovered over the next five days, until I left French Canada. If you just made the effort to speak French, even half a dozen words would do it, people would immediately relent and speak English. I spoke French when I could, but I wasn't going to risk any more over the telephone where I couldn't even lip-read.

The lady at the tourist centre asked me what sort of prices I had in mind. "What choice do I have?" I asked.

She uttered words that were to become seared into my soul over the next couple of days. "Well," she said, "there's the Château Frontenac, from one hundred to six hundred dollars a night. I don't suppose you'll want to pay that."

She was a realist. I'd already heard about the Château Frontenac, and I was to hear more. At that point I hadn't actually seen it.

We settled on Château Bellevue (just round the corner from Château Frontenac) and I went out to find a taxi.

"Château Bellevue?" I asked the driver, hopefully. His name was Georges.

He looked puzzled.

"*C'est un hotel, rue Laporte, au bord du Château Frontenac.*"

At the magic words, Château Frontenac, his brow cleared, but as he took my suitcase he said, "We speak English, *hein*?"

He had a strong French accent himself, but he was soul brother to the London cabbie ("I had Elizabeth Taylor and Richard Burton in my cab. He died soon afterwards – well, I reckon he was dead then, tell you the truth... I had Arthur Scargill in the back, address in the Barbican, that's the trouble with these Socialists, all want to live like plutocrats," etc., etc.). The Québécois version ran something like, "I had an Indian in the back of my cab. Huge guy. Head touched the roof. He says, 'I'm not going to pay you, har har.' Like, sort of, 'What are you going to do about it?' Well, I'm not a coward, but I mean ... he was joking, he did pay, but ... what *could* I have done about it?"

If we had been in London there would have been a lot more along the lines of "Hanging's too good for them, if I had my way..." but Georges, though frank in his opinions, was not the bigot I was beginning to suspect. It was clear that he was not overfond of Indians (most people I met referred to Native Americans or First Nation) mainly on the grounds that they were subject not to the local cops but only to the federal police. "Get drunk, smash things up, melt back on to the reserve, no one can identify them..."

Then he said, "But what happened at Oka, that was just asking for trouble. You don't know about Oka in England?"

As it happened, I did know about Oka, as my newspaper had carried fairly regular reports, but it hadn't struck me up to that point that here in Quebec City, Oka, by Canadian standards, was not so very far away.

What had happened at Oka, according to Georges, was that the mayor had decided to extend the golf course over land which the local Indian community regarded as sacred. When protests got them nowhere they set up an armed blockade, and when police tried to break it a corporal was killed in the resulting shoot-out. That was on 11 July. Now it was 20 September and the trouble had escalated. Whether prejudiced or not, Georges was appalled by the crassness of the golf-course incident.

The road from the airport skirted Sainte-Foy, "Where the Anglos live," said Georges, making it sound as though the English-speaking minority were also confined on some kind of reserve. As we drove into the city he said, "This is Vieux-Quebec – very like a European city." It certainly looks European in a way that Toronto, for instance, does not, but not very. Then he pointed to the right, and upwards: "Château Frontenac."

Château Frontenac – Quebec

It is impossible to take in Château Frontenac at a glance. We began to pass it, but it went on and on, up and up, towering, lowering, storey upon storey, turrets, pinnacles, dormers, gables, capped everywhere with steep green copper. Mad King Ludwig of Bavaria at his maddest never conceived anything to compare with Château Frontenac. It is as much a symbol of Quebec as Big Ben is of London, the Arc de Triomphe of Paris. It appears on poster and postcard, tea towel and table-mat, referred to always as Château Frontenac, never Hotel Château Frontenac. If you don't know that it is one of the chain of hotels built by the Canadian Pacific Railway you would assume (as possibly you are intended to) that this is a castle, a citadel, an historic monument. Oh, fair enough, it *is* an historic monument. It was built in 1893. Nearly all the old CPR hotels are impressive, in a gob-smacking way, but Château Frontenac is fabulous, in the true sense of the word. You half expect to see a thicket of impenetrable thorns growing round it, a prince climbing to an upper window by means of Rapunzel's hair, an ogre gibbering from a turret as Jack descends the beanstalk. I grew slightly tired of Château Frontenac, after a time, there is so much of it, but also fond of it, for its chutzpah as much as anything.

To reach rue Laporte and my hotel we had to drive *through* Château Frontenac, via a courtyard reached by vast gateways, and out into a sloping square, the parc des Gouverneurs. Rue Laporte ran along the top; Château Bellevue was at one end. It had, indeed, a *belle vue*; of Château Frontenac. My room was at the back on a level with the car park, and the view there was of an enormous radiator grille and a Massachusetts number plate, which never moved, all the time I was there. The room was nice, though. I unpacked, dressed to suit the weather – warmer if anything than mild Halifax – and set out to look at Quebec.

I'd been told in advance, "You can walk anywhere in Quebec." This was double-edged advice. Taken at face value it meant: Quebec is small enough to walk round (especially if you have a head for heights). It also meant: No one will be surprised if you walk. This is not to compare any Canadian city with, say, Los Angeles, where walking is said to be regarded as the recreation of perverts, criminals and the British; or with Sydney, Australia. (You walked? *Alone?*) Canadian streets are thronged with walkers. It's only when you reveal that you have walked from the bus stop or intend to walk to the subway station that eyebrows are raised. In Quebec, though, walking is positively encouraged.

There was not much traffic about. There are many places where traffic may not go, many where traffic *cannot* go. A lot of the streets are almost vertical and others have given up and become staircases. I noticed one accurately named escalier Casse-cou – Breakneck steps.

Vieux-Quebec, the old town, is the only walled city in North America. The walls around most European cities, and all British ones, are medieval. Quebec's walls were built in the nineteenth century to keep out maurauding Americans.

Enclosed by the walls at their southernmost is the Citadel. This is not the fortress commanded by Prince Edward but the one built later to plans drawn up by the Duke of Wellington. It is very like the Citadel at Halifax (which is not the one commanded by Prince Edward, either). They are both deeply entrenched. Until you are on the verge of falling over one of the sunken walls you scarcely realize that it is there. Notices were posted along the edge suggesting that it might be safer to do your rubbernecking some-where else. I turned to walk away from the lip of the fortifications and was hit in the eye by the sight of a building even bigger than Château Frontenac. It had been over there on my right ever since I walked up from rue Saint-Louis, and at first I could not think how I had failed to notice it. Staring down over the acres of green turf which are the Plains (or Heights) of Abraham, I was looking out over low, green-roofed Victorian buildings that looked rather like little outcrops of the Château. From them rose this massive modern office block, its roof laden with dishes and strung with aerials. In a sense it was monstrous, in another it literally stood alone because it was impossible to focus on *it* and on the little, low, steep-roofed, tree-girt buildings at the same time. That was how I had failed to see it. I gathered that it is a government building. It does not appear on postcards.

Judging by the number of buses parked around the perimeter we were in guided-tour country here. A party of Tic-tacs was just disembarking. I decided to give the Citadel a miss (after all, it is *very* like the one

Building site, bas – Quebec

at Halifax; seen one, seen the lot, don't you know) and turned smartly downhill on to the promenade des Gouverneurs, a broad precipitous boardwalk running down and along the steep side of Cap Diamant, that same sheer cliff *up* which General Wolfe and his army had silently hauled their artillery by night to fight the Battle of Quebec.

All I remembered of the Battle of Quebec from school history lessons was that Wolfe had commanded the English, the Marquis de Montcalm the French, and that Wolfe had said to his men, "Don't fire until you see the whites of their eyes."

We were always very impressed with this. I don't know why, unless it was by the thought of the valiant British standing there waiting for the French troops to walk to within about ten metres. If Wolfe did say it, it doesn't say much for his faith in the accuracy of the British muskets over distance.

The promenade des Gouverneurs plunged on down. Below, on the right, lay the St Lawrence – the fleuve Saint-Laurent, here – and above reared the Heights (or Plains) of Abraham. Ahead, the foothills of the Château Frontenac began to appear inexorably round the face of the bluff. When the promenade finally levelled out it was still far above the river, and far below the topmost pinnacles of the Château. This was place Dufferin, part of my hotel's *belle vue*.

Back in town, surrounded on all sides by ancient buildings, narrow streets, flights of steps, I was on the lookout for shops; not gift shops, shops. There were plenty of art galleries, gift shops, exhibitions, cafés, restaurants; what I had in mind was a drug store or the local supermarket. Rue du Tresor was lined with artists selling their work from stalls. One of them, I swear, was a reincarnation of my Canadian from the landing at school, sitting on a stool and discoursing to tourists about his paintings; easy, relaxed and with that same bottomless voice. Escalier Casse-cou was under repair so I took the long way down, a vertiginously curving road, and landed up in another beautiful ancient street – Petit-Champlain, named after the intrepid Samuel. Wall-to-wall Tic-tacs; more galleries, cafés, restaurants, gift shops. It was clear that people do actually live here, but where could they go shopping? The place was beginning to remind me more and more of Oxford, a city which, with an enormous university parked in the middle of it, has found itself squeezed into half a dozen streets in which to carry on normal life.

I went into a café, ordered coffee. At the next table two elderly ladies from Yorkshire were recording the day's expenses in dollars and cents in a small cash book and painstakingly converting everything into British currency. It was only after they'd gone that I realized I should have asked them the vital question – in English. Instead I had to ask the waitress, in French.

"*Mademoiselle, excusez-moi, mais où sont les magasins ordinaires?*"

She smiled obligingly but made some kind of French sound equivalent to "You what?"

"*Je veux trouver des magasins – l'épicier, la pharmacie –*"

She was all concern. "*Oh, vous êtes malade?*"

I ought to have broken down and confessed but pride kept me going.

"*Ah, non, mais je veux acheter des bas collants, du savon, des journaux, des pommes de terres. Où sont les magasins de la ville? Pas de touristes – pas de souvenirs...?*"

I don't know if she believed that I wanted to buy tights, soap, newspapers and potatoes, but she got the drift and immediately launched into directions in exhaustive detail, of which I understood half a dozen vital words: Château Frontenac and rue Saint-Jean.

I gathered that rue Saint-Jean lay beyond Château Frontenac (just about everything in Quebec is beyond Château Frontenac) and set out, hell-bent on finding some shops and also on losing sight of the Château. It had become a challenge.

In the côte de la Fabrique I found a chemist; at last, a sign of life. All round were Indian galleries selling native art, restaurants, *coiffures*, and *librairies* (which are not libraries but book shops), but then I found myself in the rue Saint-Jean, outside McDonalds. You had to look twice to see that it was McDonalds since it was painted a discreet green and concealed behind double doors. I can't say that I was actually pleased to see it, but it suggested that the environment was getting slightly unrespectable, and next to it was the kind of shop that we have at home on the Cowley Road, Place Zyggy's, selling earrings, brass ornaments and cheap clothes, whole garments for ten dollars. It was a far cry, if only a couple of hundred metres, from the Vieux-Quebec I was trying to escape. Further up the road was a rough pub with chipped enamelled iron tables, then a shop window full of Garfields and fridge magnets. I shouldn't have been pleased to see the same crap that I could have found in London or Oxford; I *did* appreciate the lovely pottery and paintings in Vieux-Quebec, but down here, in the rue Saint-Jean, people could actually live.

I passed a shoe shop. It was having a sale. (*Vente. 2 pour 1*) I tried to work that out; two for the price of one. Two *shoes* for the price of one?

A hot-dog shop, a pizzeria, *un dépôt nettoyeur* – the dry cleaners. My God, it *was* Cowley Road, transported across the Atlantic.

Then, suddenly, there was the city wall up ahead. The road ran under it, into the place D'Youville. Across the street the *Cinéma de Paris* was showing *Retour vers le futur III*.

Place D'Youville is a big public square, with office blocks at one end. In winter they flood it to make a skating rink. Beyond that, as far as I could see, Quebec stops being a work of art and gets on with the business of being a capital city.

The nicest thing I saw in place D'Youville was a sculpture of six Greek-type ladies on a plinth, sculpted by Alfred Laliberté. A plaque on the plinth explained that they were the Muses.

I did another quick head count. In classical mythology there are *nine* Muses, goddesses of the arts: Clio, muse of History; Melpomene, muse of Tragedy; Thalia, muse of Comedy; Euterpe, muse of Song; Erato, muse of Love Poetry; Polyhymnia, muse of Sacred Song; Calliope, muse of Epic Poetry; Urania, muse of Astronomy and Terpsichore, muse of Dance. Quebec has its own Muses: Poetry, Music, Eloquence, Architecture, Sculpture and Painting. Six is plenty, thank you very much.

I walked back down the rue Saint-Jean, pausing to visit a small supermarket; tights, soap (no newspapers or potatoes) and a submarine. Here, inland, it was just labelled *charcuterie*.

I was also on the lookout for a frog, and at last I found one. He was on a T-shirt in a shop window, clutching a Québécois flag (which is blue and white and bears *fleur-de-lis*, not a red maple leaf) and declaring: "*Grenouille. Et fière de l'être*." A frog, and proud to be one. He was a separatist.

It was only while cruising round a museum the following day that I discovered that here, Wolfe's victory over Montcalm and the subsequent British takeover is still referred to as The Conquest, and there has always been a feeling that the province of Quebec should be independent of British Canada. This feeling flared into violence in the 1970s and in 1976 the separatist *Parti Québécois* won a majority in the Provincial Assembly, holding a referendum four years later on whether Quebec should remain a part of Canada. It *has* remained a part of Canada – so far.

Quebec night-life is famous, but rain and darkness were falling when I got back to Château Bellevue; I decided to give the night-life a miss and settled down with the submarine to see what Quebec could provide in the way of television. Most of what was on offer was in French, which is now the official language of the province. As with *Back to the Future III*, a film, upon release in Quebec, has sixty days in which to get itself dubbed into French, otherwise it is withdrawn. A fascinating news item showed two actors, a man and a woman, dubbing a violently passionate love scene. They stood primly, side by side, enthusiastically kissing not each other but the insides of their own elbows to get the authentic squelch of what was happening in English on the screen. "Sometimes we work eighteen hours a day," they claimed modestly, and fell to gnawing their inner arms again.

The news, which was in English, was mainly about the events at Oka. There was more to the Oka affair now than just the golf-course incident. After the storming of the original blockade at Oka itself, Mohawks from the Kahnawake Reserve, near Montreal, had barricaded the busy Mercier Bridge into Montreal city, threatening to blow it up if the police made another raid at Oka. One end of the bridge is in Mohawk territory. A month later, in the middle of August, violence broke out when thousands of furious commuters, denied access to the bridge, demonstrated against the blockade and police intervened with batons and tear-gas. The bridge had finally been "liberated" and at the beginning of September the army had torn down the barricades at Oka. Now the last of the Mohawk Warriors and their supporters were holed up in a detoxification treatment centre on the reserve. There was a general feeling that the end was near, but that this was a problem that was not about to be solved. Indians right across the country were laying formal claims to land which they regarded as rightfully theirs. Sources in the government said that they amounted to three quarters of the entire country. A journalist remarked sourly that if all the claims were met, Canada would end up looking like a Gruyère cheese.

It was an unhappy business; unhappy for the Mohawks, unhappy for the Canadians, aghast at seeing violence on this scale in their own country. Whenever I spoke to anyone about it, the *un*spoken protest was always there: "How can this have happened? We aren't *like* this."

I switched on the news again next morning, for an update on Oka, but had mislaid the channel. Instead I got a French-language second-hand shop, which was an improvement even on the used-car channel in Halifax. A selection of goods was shown on the screen, one after another, while a voice-over read out prices and details. On offer were: a carbine, a vacuum cleaner, a mobile home, a car, a plot of building land with several birch trees *in situ*, a house, a ski chalet to let, a set of double doors, a piano and – a kitchen sink.

It was a beautiful morning. I went down to a little café in rue Saint-Louis that specialized in serving *le petit déjeuner* and was full of Americans eating English breakfasts, and then lit out for the post office, where the mail boxes are firmly anchored in the wall and therefore unable to escape. Across the street is the parc Montmorency, standing right on the lip of the precipice above the St Lawrence. Down below, a sheer drop, was the port; beyond the roofs of buildings I could see a ship at anchor and went down to investigate, along a winding bob-sleigh-run of a street called Côte de la Montaigne. Round the corner and across the street I saw what I thought at first must be a vast new hotel, all glass and stone. It turned out to be a museum, *Musée de la Civilisation*. I went in, intending a quick look round. After two hours I had looked round only one exhibit, *Mémoires*, a history of Quebec province. It was impressive by any standards, but the most memorable memoir was right at the beginning. A winding road led through dark forests in the snow. It was all done with clever lighting and cardboard, but the silence, the eerie shadows, worked magic. In moments I had forgotten the huge glass and stone edifice above; forgotten that this was an exhibit in a well-heated museum. I too was in old Quebec; lost; cold. When a family came in chatting, I heard their approaching footsteps with something like shock and moved on, almost disappointed. Beyond lay progress, to the present day: light domestic interiors, machines, farm equipment, printing presses ... it was all magnificent, but I had left my imagination in the forest. One startling item of information adhered; in old Quebec society, the local priest was responsible for educating a family's *twenty-sixth* child.

In the atrium of the museum was a great stone pool with large rocks disposed in it. From time to time I saw children nip over the wall for a quick paddle – and for another reason. The basin was full of coins. There was once a film called *Three Coins in the Fountain*, the fountain in question being the Trevi in Rome, with its legend that if you throw a coin into it your wish will be granted. The idea has spread. People the world over seem to have an urge to throw money into water – any water. There must be a small fortune lying on the bottom of the pool in the *Musée de la Civilisation*. Small wet footprints led away from it in all directions. Occasionally a member of staff intervened, probably for safety reasons, I decided, after going down to the basement for coffee. One side of the basin dropped sheerly away and the water ran down it in a glistening sheet. There were no tiny corpses in the trough at the foot of the drop, but many more little wet prints.

After that it was back up the Côte de la Montaigne and into rue Saint-Jean to collect the evening meal and then into an Indian gallery. I wanted to buy some wild rice, which is truly wild, although not truly rice but grass seed, harvested by hand and hideously expensive, even in Canada. These galleries, and there are many, specialize in selling Indian and Inuit art. I discovered some time ago that the Canadian Eskimos, tired of being described by a word that means, basically, "they-eat-raw-meat", had persuaded the world to use their own name for themselves – Inuit, meaning simply, the people. I have never heard a Canadian speak of Eskimos.

The Indian and Inuit artefacts for sale in the galleries were beautiful, but involved a lot of fur. It is hard to be pious about fur in a country which was founded on trapping and where the winter temperatures are deeply subzero, but I didn't feel that I wanted to bring any back with me. I'd already noticed signs in airports advising US citizens that they would not be permitted to bring certain skins back into the United States.

Round the corner from the gallery, in rue

Donnacona, I found a chapel. I was actually looking for the museum of the Ursuline nuns, but it was just about to close for the night, and next to it was their convent. The chapel was in the public part, and through a screen beside the altar I could see the nuns in their own chapel, proper nuns in coif and wimple, motionless in their stalls. A crabby concierge bustled about driving trespassing tourists away from the sisters' private quarters.

The chapel is barely a century old, but everything inside is taken from the chapel that stood on the site before, built in the eighteenth century. It was finished in 1736, and twenty-three years later, after the Battle of Quebec, General Montcalm was buried here, in a bomb crater in the floor. An imposing stone memorial tablet was fixed to the wall above his resting place, but others had been added, by more recent admirers and sympathizers.

HOMAGE DES SAINT-CYRIENS
AU MARQUIS DE MONTCALM
1982 – FRANCE

HONNEUR
à
MONTCALM
La destine en lui dérobant
La Victoire
L'a recompencé par
Une Mort Glorieuse!

Coming in I had noticed a sign in French on one of

the double doors. Going out I saw the English translation on the other door.

THIS CHAPEL IS PLACE TO PRAY
SILENCE PLEASE
RESPECTUOUS CLOTHES REQUIRED

Now I understood the old lady's outrage when she drove the giggling backpackers out of the nuns' chapel. Their clothes had not been at all respectuous.

On the way back to the Château I dropped in at Musée de Cire, the wax museum. If it had looked anything like Madame Tussaud's I'd have crossed the street to avoid it, but this was just a tall house, near the Anglican Cathedral (which is said to be modelled on St Martin in the Fields), offering a history of the province on three floors, in a series of tableaux of wax models. The earliest exhibits, near the entrance, featured valiant founding Québécoises, signing documents, building settlements, repelling Iroquois warriors. Wolfe wrote his last letter on the eve of battle; Montcalm died; Wolfe died; various Iroquois died. The sculptor was ace at death throes. In most of the tableaux the liveliest figure was usually the one who was expiring on the floor.

The final scene, which occupied most of the top floor, was entitled "The Gathering of Savants" and assembled the great minds of the modern world in a dreary drawing-room. They looked like people who had arrived too early for a party. Marie Curie was there, Edison, Einstein, Churchill, Field Marshal Montgomery and William Lyon Mackenzie King.

I was about to leave when I noticed, by the door, a curious group, unfinished, unlit and lurking. Behind the glass stood what looked like two of the Vatican's Swiss Guards, and between them a short lunatic in modern dress, with rolling eyes. It was exactly at this moment that I became aware of strange sounds overhead, a muffled trundling.

Downstairs again I asked the girl at the desk what this tableau represented. She said she didn't know who they were and added that she, personally, did not care to go up there alone at night.

I thought of those strange sounds from above. Hadn't I been on the *top* floor?

That evening I followed more of the Oka siege on television. Denis Trudeau, the anchor man, was interviewing Chief Joe Norton, the Mohawk leader, a genial type in a blue lounge suit, about some alarming claims made by the police on the subject of Mohawk weaponry and general conduct; claims very much at odds with Chief Joe's version.

"Some might say you're both lying," said Denis, bluntly.

"Depends who sounds the most credible, then," said Chief Joe, with a disarming smile. Shortly afterwards we were treated to a live harangue from the army commander who was about to take control. I thought back to Chief Joe Norton's comment and decided that he had a point. There was no doubt about whom one would *rather* believe. All the while there was this sense of seismic national shock, not just that it had happened, but that it had happened in Canada. *We aren't like this.*

After the news there was a choice of Prince Charles in English or James Bond in French. I watched James Bond for a bit, trying to decide if Roger Moore had been dubbed or if he was just out of sync, but given the dialogue in James Bond movies, it didn't matter much anyway. They could have been speaking Hungarian for all the difference it made.

Next morning I lugged my suitcases through the courtyard of Château Frontenac for the last time, and took a cab to the bus station. I was agog to see the bus station. What would it look like – the Louvre? The taxi left Château Frontenac far behind and downtown Quebec closed round us. We were in the hinterland of place D'Youville. Quebec bus station looked just like any other bus station. Name it – you've been there. I felt very at home. It was cleaner than its English counterpart – inevitably – but, a bus station is a bus station. And the Voyageur, Canadian version of the celebrated American Greyhound bus, was just a bus; that is, a coach: clean, comfortable, with a loo at the back, but still a coach.

After we left the suburbs of Quebec the view became very East Anglian, very flat, very dull. After fifteen years of living in Norfolk I can take only so much sky. I slept all the way to Montreal.

Chapter Four

My first sight of Montreal was of trees and hills and what looked like a gigantic upturned wok with a detachable handle. This, though I didn't know it at the time, may be the source of Canada's deep suspicion of things large and technical. Built for the '76 Olympics it was an all-weather sports stadium, the wok being the stadium and the handle an immense concrete structure from which the roof could be lifted. "It stuck," Bill, my host, told me later. I tactlessly compared it with the non-stick dome in Toronto. "Ha," said Bill. "The difference between French design and Canadian engineering."

I hadn't realized, until I saw it, that Montreal is an island in the St Lawrence, and that in the centre of the city, whose name means Mount Royal, there really is a mountain – called Mount Royal. We crossed bridges to reach the city itself, although not the Mercier Bridge which lies further upstream, to the west. We crossed a smaller island on the way. Floating incredibly above the treetops was a great soap bubble, like a geodetic sphere. It *is* a geodetic sphere, the United States' pavilion left over from Expo '67, which had subsequently caught fire. These things are rarely more than impressive. Burned out and transparent, this one is beautiful. Almost I expected it to drift away, and up, over the mountain.

Bill and Esther met me at the bus station. I was to stay with them in Westmount (where the Anglos live), *Lower* Westmount, as they explained, as we drove round the city. Upper Westmount is where the nobs hang out, and clings elegantly to the side of the mountain.

Montreal began with lunch; souvlaki in a Greek restaurant on rue Saint-Urbain. It was opposite a Jewish bakery, where matzohs and bagels were being made. From where we sat we could see across the street to the flaring ovens as the bagels were lifted out on long paddles. After lunch we went over to buy some. On the counter, matzohs lay in heaps. The only matzohs I had seen before were the kind you can buy here, in boxes; large, pale, perforated crackers. These were the real thing, the unleavened bread that the Jews hurriedly made before Moses led them out of Egypt; unleavened because they dared not wait for it to rise.

The bakery smelled wonderful; the queue went out on to the street. It was Saturday, the Sabbath. Past the window walked Orthodox Jewish families; little girls in long bunchy frocks, men in wide, gingery fur hats, called *shtreimels*.

Westmount is not far from the city centre – later I walked it – but we took the scenic route home, over the mountain. Bill explained that part of it is sacred to the Indians. Esther pointed out that much of it is now a cemetery. My interest was instantly aroused. Tomorrow, I promised myself, I would have my graveyard fix.

But there were other things to be done first. Bill dropped me off at the Central Station to book my seat for the next leg of the journey to Belleville, Ontario. Here, it seemed, taking a train was not a matter of arriving at the station at the last minute and buying a ticket. Catching an inter-city train in Canada is more like arranging an airline flight. The ticket itself is like an airline ticket, in a little folder with regulations printed on it. While I was queuing, urban Montreal raised its dangerous head. Three fat yobbos surged on to the concourse and began shoving barriers around. This was the first sign of Canadian disorder I'd ever seen. Were they about to riot? They looked the kind who get automatically moved on by policemen. No; shoving the barriers about was the sum of their outlawry, to indicate their contempt for queues. After a few minutes they put the barriers back tidily and joined the queue.

Nevertheless, there was an air of danger about Montreal. It was hard to put a finger on; there were no threatening crowds, no distant gunshots, no signs of murder and mugging on the streets. In the end I put it down to the traffic and the Montrealers themselves. For a start, the traffic was thicker and faster than anything I had encountered so far. For the first time ever in Canada, I became aware of the possibility of being run over. In Quebec you have to walk quite a long way in order to get run down. In Toronto you would have to leap out in front of a

truck with malice aforethought. I once saw a taxi in
Toronto skid on an oil slick in the rain and turn three
hundred and sixty degrees on one wheel. I cowered
in a doorway, waiting for the carnage, but there was
so much street, so little traffic, all of it moving
sedately, that no other vehicle was even touched and
the taxi, recovering its composure, glided on.
Torontonians would probably gape at the suggestion
that they don't have much traffic – if they haven't
been to London, that is.

Even so, the traffic in Montreal didn't seem to be
all *that* savage. In my book on eastern Canada it says
tersely, "The Montreal police are not tolerant of
traffic violations." Finally I realized that the sense of
peril, of lawlessness at pedestrian crossings, was due
solely to the pedestrians. I could hardly believe it.
They don't wait for the WALK signal. Instead they
surge out into the road, no doubt confident of
vengeful cops if they do get flattened.

I was on my way to McGill College to view a piece
of sculpture. This was not McGill University, but the
street named after the original college, founded by
one James McGill in the eighteenth century. It
became a university in 1821 and one of its Life
Governors was Peter McGill, a relative of the
founder. He was also president of the Montreal Bank,
mayor of Montreal, speaker of the Legislative
Council of Canada and president of the Board of
Trade. His grandson was also distinguished; in a way.
He was an Englishman, Donald McGill, who made
his name by illustrating naughty seaside postcards.

The sculpture I was going to see is formally entitled

la foule illuminée. Esther, who had told me that I should on no account miss it, called it the butterscotch sculpture. Not wanting to spoil my surprise she had not described it in detail, but she needn't have worried. *La foule illuminée* is virtually indescribable.

Unlike Europeans, the Canadians don't go in for equestrian statues, kings, generals and wild women in chariots. There are not many politicians about, either, although Norene had told me of a statue to a successful financier whose boot toe was brightly polished by people touching it for luck. Admittedly Montreal is full of angels, they crop up all over the place, but on the whole public sculpture is what you might call eccentric. From the statue of Winston Churchill in Halifax, to the Italian war memorial in Toronto, known as The Gumbie, to the giant Inukshuk in Vancouver, no one piece bears any relation to another. *La foule illuminée* bears no relation to anything.

Forewarned about the butterscotch effect I spotted *la foule* from the other side of the street. "The crowd", all sculpted in some pale yellow substance, possibly a petrified form of polyunsaturated fat, stands in the entrance to the Banque Laurentienne and stares across the road at a tall building on the other side. One of them points ... at something. From a western aspect the crowd looks, except for its colour, like a group of tourists; a group of tourists who have been walking for hours and don't much care for what they have come to see. They do not look happy. Then you notice that beside the man who points, someone has collapsed and is crouching at the feet of the others. You continue to prowl round it. The crowd goes downhill, physically and metaphorically. Civilization declines and all hell breaks loose at the back; here are men fighting, a corpse, a cloud of smoke, the Ku Klux Klan; all in that same strange, repellent shade of pale yellow. I was glad I'd never seen *la foule illuminée* in childhood. It is the stuff of nightmares, and I liked it a lot.

I saw one other marvel on avenue McGill College; a mail box being emptied. I stood a while and stared, to make sure it was really happening. The mail box was at a disadvantage, though, being legless and cemented to the pavement. It was like shooting a sitting duck.

At the end of McGill I turned left on to Sherbrooke, where the private art galleries and posh-frock shops are. A small mild rain was falling. In common with the Canadian practice of sharing whatever's going, the art galleries, although by now closed for the night, exhibited many sculptures outside on the pavement, a bronze by Rodin rubbing shoulders with modern Canadian pieces, some of them explicit enough to have got them moved into a discreet corner in England where, at about the same time, a statue of a nude man, an entirely blameless nude man, had become known as the Rude Man of Lincoln, after members of the public had complained about its being exhibited in the cathedral there. Outside one building, apparently the headquarters of the strangely named Madikap organization, were three cut-outs, of a man, a woman and a dog, ornamented with details that would have invited prosecution in London. I saw no evidence of Montrealers dropping in their tracks from moral outrage.

On the far side of the road stood two buildings that reminded me of Kentish oast houses; stony cylindrical walls, pointed slaty roofs. These are Indian towers, where the earliest settlers would retreat when under threat of attack from the locals. Built in 1676, they are possibly the oldest surviving buildings in Canada. Those earliest settlers were missionaries. Montreal is still full of great stone buildings that were once monasteries, convents, seminaries. Now they are hospitals, schools, colleges, but a reminder that the city, until the 1960s, was heavily under the hand of the Roman Catholic Church. It still has more cathedrals to the square mile than most cities. I'd already caught a glimpse of one of them down near the station, Marie-Reine-du-Monde, a scaled-down version of St Peter's in Rome. Dwarfed among the skyscrapers it looked more scaled down than ever, and charming; a dolls' cathedral. The following day I saw a less charming one, but more of that later.

I heard it said at various times that Montreal has five seasons – spring, summer, fall, winter and construction; and that Montreal has two seasons – winter and construction. This probably applies to most of Canada. There was certainly a lot of construction going on all around, but it is quite possible to live in Montreal and experience no seasons at all. Under the surface is another city, Montreal Souterrain, where you can live, work, travel, shop, eat out, visit the theatre, without ever surfacing. This sounded advanced and sensible – and also slightly creepy.

On the other hand, I wasn't seeing Montreal in winter.

Next day I headed for the cemetery, Notre-Dame de la Côte des Neiges, high up on Mount Royal. There was, inevitably, an angel guarding the entrance. I passed by her, walking across the turf, upwards, to the street of mausoleums. These are bigger, darker, gloomier than the mausoleums in Toronto. Some had furniture inside. One boasted enough chairs and a table big enough for a board meeting. Helpful signs directed visitors to the choicer exhibits. It was warm,

"Notre-Dame de la Côte des Neiges" – Montreal

sunny, peaceful. People walked among the trees, taking a Sunday morning stroll. Notre-Dame is a necropolis in the truest sense, a city of the dead and, like a real city, it has suburbs.

Leaving the mausoleums I walked on, and up. Ahead of me, on the hill crest, was a little wood, and below it a grassy field, only roughly mown and, as far as I could see, unused. Perhaps it awaited a landscape gardener, for the rest of the cemetery was beautifully maintained. I began to cross the field, paying no particular attention to where I was treading, until I felt stone under my shoe and noticed a block of white marble, perhaps a foot square, lying half covered in long grass. There was only one word on it: *enfant.* Nearby lay another, and another: *enfant ... enfant.* I began to look more closely. Here and there a little stone stood upright, like a first tooth; *enfant ... enfant ... enfant.* This was the crèche, where the babies were laid. I wondered at the neglect, compared with the clipped turf and pruned shrubs of the lower slopes where the grown-ups rested, but that was unthinkable. In an English graveyard, yes, maybe; very likely; but here? The field lay on a south-facing slope. It must be filled with wild flowers in summer. Perhaps that is where the really little children would rather be, all together in this sunny meadow.

The last grave I saw there was on the further side, near the trees. Raymond Savant, three months old. It seemed to tell a story of poverty and devotion, for Raymond's memorial was home-made. Was his papa a plumber? It was a cross, welded together out of copper water-pipes. To it was fixed a small sheet of aluminium on which an inscription had been tapped with a nail point: *Raymond Savant Né Janvier 1959 Déc Avril*. Later on, I saw little Raymond had been given a proper stone, but his pipework cross still stood.

The suburb on the summit was a new one, the headstones close together in regular rows, back to back, like terraced town houses. Geraniums bloomed in the front gardens. It was a terribly respectable neighbourhood, except for a gang of tearaway chipmunks who were belting up and down an alley-way between the backs of the stones. In the distance loomed the aerials and transmitters of the police headquarters that sits watchfully on top of Mount Royal.

It was a long walk to the subway station. I thought I might stop off for coffee somewhere, but all the while I was walking down the slope of Côte des Neiges, to the gate, I could see beyond some trees a green copper dome, high on an adjacent hillside. I'd caught a glimpse of this the day before as we drove over the mountain. "St Joseph's Oratory," Bill had told me. "It's erected over the shrine of Brother André. Built with the pennies of the poor."

The pennies of the poor. I'd imagined something charmingly ramshackle with, perhaps, the dome balanced insecurely on top. Brother André sounded a modest type. I expected his shrine to match, envisaging a climb through the woods to reach the oratory – which must have been the case, once. Following a signpost I turned down a side street and began at once to suspect that I'd got it wrong. Across the end of the street were uncompromising iron gates. I saw cars, people; dozens of cars, hundreds of people. I reached the gates. I turned and looked. And looked.

Up. It was enormous, on the summit of a crag reached by sweeping roads and ninety-nine steps. The steps went up in rows of three and the central row was cordoned off with a notice affixed to the barrier:

RÉSERVÉ
AUX PÈLERINS QUI MONTENT À GENOUX

There were at the time no pilgrims who were ascending on their knees, and most people took the roadway as opposed to those mountainous steps, but the sign made me remember that this was not simply the tomb of Brother André, but his shrine, a place of pilgrimage – were miracles performed here?

The oratory was entered via the crypt. As I went in the smell of hot wax was sticky, almost tangible. On either side rose banks of votive lights, in white, red and green glass; the colour, I discovered, advertised the amount you had paid, dollars or cents. And from floor to ceiling hung crutches, rows and rows of crutches, of the kind displayed at Lourdes, ostensibly left behind by those who had been lame and were now cured and who, presumably, went bounding back down the steps on their own two feet. I looked long and hard and suspiciously at those crutches. They were as near as dammit identical, small and made of wood; the kind of crutches used by cripples in paintings by Brueghel the Elder. Brother André died only half a century ago; I hadn't seen crutches like that used in my lifetime.

A small doorway bore a sign indicating that through here was the tomb of Brother André. It led into a low, horseshoe-shaped passage, very quiet and still. Halfway round was a plain black stone table tomb, wherein André lay. Two men, each with one hand to his face, the other laid flat upon the stone slab, prayed in silence. I walked past, silently, and back out into the crypt, to the crutches, the hot wax, the dollars and cents.

To reach the main basilica, escalators had been installed. I wondered briefly if pilgrims attempted to ascend the escalators on their knees. The nave was dimly lit and crushingly crowded. Mass, conducted at the brilliantly illuminated altar at one end, looked like a stage performance. When it ended, with a flourish, I half expected the audience to break into applause.

I walked up one aisle and then out again. That was enough. Outside, beneath the dome, the view across Montreal was rain-washed and astonishing but not, I felt, enough of an antidote to what was going on inside. I went down again, and left without making a donation, although I understand that the place still isn't completed, and ashamed of unworthy thoughts. But I reckoned it had swallowed enough donations already: the pennies of the poor.

How many pennies, for God's sake? *How* poor?

Outside the subway a young man was begging on the street.

The Montreal subway is called, Paris fashion, the

Metro. The stations are clean, the trains run on rubber wheels. How unlike the infamous New York Subway, I thought. How unlike our own dear London Underground. It was almost empty, too. I felt a stab of nostalgia when I saw an escalator that was out of action, but it was Sunday, so they were probably cleaning it. I doubted very much that it would still be out of commission next day or, like one of ours, the following month.

The station at Champ-de-Mars debouched into the lower reaches of rue Saint-Urbain, in a rainstorm. Beneath the pounding of the rain I could hear a threatening, continuous growl. Over a surprisingly low parapet lay an unguarded drop to the autoroute beneath. Supposing children toppled over, or suicides jumped? I thought, recalling the kindly concern of the Halifax Waterfront Corporation for the safety of its errant skateboarders. The view in Montreal appeared to be along the lines of: If you are fool enough to climb about on this wall you deserve to break your neck.

On the far side of the autoroute lay Vieux-Montreal. To the west the skyscrapers stood in a rampart, but the last of the tall buildings was the Cathedral of Notre-Dame, grey and forbidding without, inside glowing red, indigo, violet, like one of those brooches made of butterflies' wings. The road ran downhill beside the cathedral and suddenly out on to the waterfront. Across the road, on quai King Edward, a warehouse the size of an airship hangar proclaimed itself *Flea market*.

Ever a sucker for flea markets I went in. The place

was filled with stalls, selling everything from outright junk to genuine, although not necessarily desirable, antiques. There was food and farm produce too. Some people, like me, were browsing; others seriously shopping. Among them strode an ecclesiastical person, so wonderfully robed and decorated that it was impossible to guess which religion he represented. He looked like the high priest of some arcane rite of a pagan creed. I tried to follow him but there was so much else to look at and so many people. Crowds closed behind his scarlet garments. Later I came across him at the far end of the market and had time to notice that a cross hung from his neck, so presumably he was some kind of a Christian. He was propped up against a refreshment stall, drinking coffee from a paper cup and chatting to the proprietor.

Crossing the street to reach the flea market I'd been abstractedly aware of walking over railway lines. On the way out, I saw a locomotive ... a train. We were some way from the main line station so I went to investigate. There was a long queue waiting to board the train, a very long queue, curling round the outside of a marquee from which issued the sound of New Orleans jazz. This was not any old train; this was the famous stainless steel train of 1955, pride of the Canadian Pacific transcontinental route, the one that had just come to an ignominious end at the orders of the government and much against the wishes of the population. It had been restored to its former glory, redecorated, lined with murals by distinguished Canadian painters – but it wasn't going anywhere. The queue was waiting to *see* it, not travel on it.

There is still a service across Canada, three days a week, but it follows a duller, cheaper route than it used to, and people speak of it in shamed tones. After all, the CPR first built that line through the Rockies to link British Columbia to the rest of Canada and so coax it to join the other provinces. I didn't join the queue.

That evening we watched on television the first episode of a series about the American Civil War. It was impressively done, and timely, as the announcer pointed out before transmission began; timely for Canada, that is. This war, she explained, had been fought to keep a nation together. Canada, in imminent danger of disintegration, take note. People spoke so often of the fear that when – rather than if – Quebec seceded, the rest of the country would fall apart. The thread that had held together that necklace of disparate provinces, the CPR, had been severed. Bureaucrats, PR men, spokespersons, politicians piped up from time to time, to explain that really it was a good thing; good for the railway; good for Canada.

I never met a Canadian who believed this.

Chapter Five

Now I was heading west again, back into Ontario, to Prince Edward County.

The train left at ten-thirty. I got there in good time and joined the queue. The British like to believe that they are the only people in the world who know how to queue because they learned to do it *properly*, during World War Two, but Canadians do it just as well as we do. This queue led to the head of the steps that went down from the station concourse to the track for, I discovered, here you do not hang around on the platform and hurl yourself at the train when the moment comes. It was, as I had thought the day I bought the ticket, far more like boarding an aircraft. The ticket was only the beginning. This was checked in the queue, then baggage handlers came by to take on board large items. The ticket was checked again on the platform and I was directed to my seat, in a particular car. Inside it was warm, wide, comfortable, clean. A couple behind me were complaining about the age of the rolling stock. You don't know you're born, I thought. Come to London and experience the joys of travelling on a Southern Region commuter train. You North Americans love antiques, don't you? Why, some of our rolling stock is sixty years old. But I didn't say anything. It was too long a trip to risk making enemies before we even left the station.

The ticket was checked again by the conductor – the novelty was wearing off by now – and the destination affixed to the luggage rack overhead, presumably so that he could look out for sleeping, dishonest or deranged passengers who had overshot their station.

The train left on time. I was fit to be impressed by everything by now, but on the other hand, there was no reason why it shouldn't leave on time. I had noticed on the concourse that the whole of the day's trains could be fitted on to a single timetable. While we'd queued for the Toronto train, posted for ten-thirty, I'd looked around and seen the next one posted on an adjacent platform; to leave at five-thirty.

Oh, and then came the sound, the real and true sound of the North American railway, the prairie locomotive, the plaintive whistle of a thousand Westerns, heralding High Noon or the 3.10 to Yuma. Admittedly we were only ten minutes out of the station when I heard it first, and it took another half hour to clear the suburbs, but it is a thrilling sound, more like the moan of a giant harmonica than a whistle, and nothing like the hee-hawing Klaxons of British Rail, a most desolate sound. Hear that lonesome whistle blow.

At last we left Montreal behind and drew on through woodland and scrub and open plain, out on to the Canadian Shield. Bill had told me that we would be crossing it, and from time to time I looked up from my copy of *The New Yorker* (a greatly overrated magazine) in the hope of seeing it, the real thing. Because, you must understand, I once learned about the Canadian Shield in geography lessons at school. That is, Geography was taught in my presence; I learned very little, being more occupied with drawing pictures on the blotting paper; this was in the Dark Ages when we used ink. A few things stuck, though; the Ganges delta, the Notts/Derby coalfield, sisal production in East Africa, the Canadian Shield. All I recalled of it was a meaningless shape, heavily shaded, in a textbook, which had then to be traced into an exercise book. If you showed me now maps of the Canadian Shield and the Notts/Derby coalfield, I doubt very much if I could tell you which was which. I remember, when I first travelled to the English industrial Midlands, Nottingham and Derbyshire, looking out of the window of the train, seeing the winding gear at the pit heads and thinking, My God! This is *it*. The Notts/Derby coalfield. *It exists*. Now I looked out of the train and thought, This is it! The Canadian Shield. Not that I would have known if Bill hadn't told me. It didn't bear much resemblance to my sketch maps. The Shield is rock, immensely ancient pre-Cambrian rock. Now and again I spotted a grey hump, like the quarters of a slumbering mammoth, looming out of the turf.

I was still hoping for a sight of the famous fall colours, the rich, incredible scarlets and crimsons, vermilions and golds of the north-east of the American continent. Here and there were signs, a patch of brilliant sumac, but then all was green again.

I had, of course, chosen the *wrong year* to see the fall. The first time I visited Canada I was too late, the second time, too early. This year I'd got the timing right but the weather was wrong. For true fall splendour you need warm days and cold nights. We were having warm*ish* days and cold*ish* nights. Fall looked like an English autumn.

I began to notice the sleeping elephants after we left Brockville. Almost due north of Brockville is Ottawa, the capital of all Canada, chosen in 1857 by Queen Victoria because it wasn't the capital of anywhere else. I didn't have time to visit Ottawa, and this was the closest I got to it. It looks, from photographs, like an attractive town, but from my point of view its chief interest lay in the fact that it was for a time the home of Archibald Lampman, who worked in the post office and loved frogs.

I doubt if this is how he would have wished to be remembered. He was a serious poet, who did not particularly want to work in the post office. Instead he dreamed of being able to live in the country and write his poetry undisturbed. The year before he died, he wrote, "I wish I had a little cottage in some sunny mountainous land with nothing to do but cultivate a small garden and make a few poems now and then." He was a melancholy man and knew, and feared, that many of the things he loved were already passing. Almost a hundred years ago he wrote: "Not only are our magnificent pine forests disappearing, not only is the buffalo practically extinct and the wild pigeon rapidly becoming so, but wherever any wild thing of interest or beauty occurs in rare haunts it is instantly set upon and destroyed."

It has taken the rest of the world a long time to catch up with Lampman. He wrote a fairy tale about Hans Fingerhut, an angry poet, who was turned into a frog – not as a punishment, Lampman thought too highly of frogs for that – but so that he might learn to understand the song of a stream. "He heard the innumerable voices of the frogs, at first sharp and fitful and at last swelling into a steady thunder far away down the stream..." Lampman was writing of thousands of frogs. Now their numbers are said to be dwindling.

He also wrote a poem called "Favourites of Pan" – about frogs. It tells of the time when Christianity drove away the old classical gods of Greece with "hostile hymns and conquering faiths". Pan, the great goat-footed nature god, fled with the others, stopping only to cut fresh reeds for his pipes, or syrinx. And when he played, all the frogs came out round about him on the wet cool earth. Pan lifted them up, one by one, and blew gently into their mouths:

> And ever from that hour the frogs repeat
> The murmur of Pan's pipes, the notes
>   And answers strange and sweet.

> And they that hear them are renewed
>   By knowledge in some god-like touch
>   conveyed,
> Entering again into the eternal mood
>   Wherein the world was made.

He wrote a poem called "The Frogs" too, calling them "flutists", with voices high and strange. These are definitely not the frogs that we think of as lumping about in swamps and croaking, "Ribbet, ribbet". The word "croak" is never mentioned in connection with Canadian frogs.

Ottawa, being the capital, contains the Houses of Parliament and is, consequently, full of politicians. And so it was in 1894 when Lampman wrote, in a letter to his friend E. W. Thomson:

I see a number of members of parliament prowling about today. What are they after? Vipers, bloodsuckers! Whenever I see the national collection of cut-purses and bunco men gathering together here, my mind returns with love and admiring tenderness to the figure of poor old Guy Fawkes – certainly one of the most venerable heroes in English history – for to him occurred the one luminous idea the gravest that ever fired the brain of any Briton – that of placing a great many barrels of gunpowder under the Houses of Parliament and blowing the whole lot of them to Kingdom come at one fell bang. What a glorious idea was that. Poor, imaginative, patriotic Old Guy. If I had my way I would canonise him St Fawkes! St Guido of Westminster. Sly old villainous Guy who wanted to murder the king, that James I. Of course he did! No sensible man could have harboured any other purpose in regard to such a ridiculous vexatious old popinjay as James I.

I think I must write an ode to Guy Fawkes.
Did you get your moose's head through?

He went a little over the top on the matter of Guy
Fawkes, and it is hard to imagine sad, gentle
Lampman blowing up anyone himself. And Mr
Thomson's moose's head?

Probably still languishing in a mail box, somewhere.

At eleven twenty-five there appeared among us
François, our service manager. He was superb, in grey
trousers and waistcoat, slender, elegant, with a
sculpted blond coiffure. He was also charming, asked
courteously if there were any Francophones in the
car. There was an almost abashed murmur of dissent.
It seemed ineffably boorish to admit that none of us
was.

"*Non?* Everyone's English?" He introduced
himself and explained that we should seek him out to
complain if all was not as we desired. I couldn't
imagine needing to address any complaints to
François. Long after he had moved on to the next car
his exquisite shade lingered in the aisle, a mute
rebuke to the disembodied voice on British Rail that
announces, brusquely, "This is you senior conductor
speaking," and informs you, after the train has left the
station, that concessionary tickets are not valid on this
service.

A kind of airline meal was served, in our seats, all
included in the ticket price. Eat your heart out,
Travellers Fare, I thought savagely, tearing into a
mini-submarine. The drinks trolley followed. I

relaxed, put aside *The New Yorker* and opened the *Globe and Mail*; skimmed the headlines and then turned to the back page which regularly features a column entitled *Social Studies*.

This is a jolly rag-bag of facts, sometimes all unconnected, sometimes on a theme. On the day I arrived in Toronto it had carried a collection of all the statistics you didn't want to know about airline fatalities. There was an interesting item today relating to air travel as well, culled from an American newspaper. Apparently airline staff are becoming deeply suspicious of passengers with heavy garment bags. The garment bag is a kind of portable wardrobe in which you can hang up your suit or posh frock without creasing it. It seems that sometimes they turn out to contain not garments but corpses. Since the cost of transporting a dead body the conventional way, in a coffin, has become prohibitive, thrifty relatives have been known to zip Uncle into a garment bag and, one assumes, hang him up in a locker at the rear of the plane. The airline spokesman, with commendable understanding, was reported to have remarked that it *was* very difficult to stuff a corpse into an overhead locker.

It seemed to be getting dark outside. I looked out of the window. We were passing a freight train. About thirty seconds later I looked up again. We were still passing it. Now, at level crossings, lasting friendships can be formed while a Canadian freight train goes by. My train was moving at about fifty kilometres an hour and so, by the look of it, was the freight train, but it still took over a minute before we were past each other. It had three locomotives at the rear. I wished I'd looked up in time to see how many it had at the front. I once saw a freight train in the Rockies with three in the middle.

The *Globe and Mail* also carried a review of a movie, *Narrow Margin*, much of which, it appeared, took place on a Canadian passenger train. The critic remarked sardonically upon the fact that in several scenes the train *stopped* at *stations* and *people got on and off.* "Ain't that a wild stretch of fictional fancy?" he enquired.

This made me look out at stations and take notice. At every one, large numbers of grannies seemed to be boarding, seen off by waving families.

The train began stopping between stations, once ... twice. No one seemed to mind very much, or be very surprised. After all, we were now travelling so slowly that stopping made very little difference.

I wasn't complaining. Recently I travelled on a train from London to Liverpool. It was extremely fast and extremely filthy. Two of the coaches had no heat and two no light. You could take your pick. Secure in the knowledge that I was going to be able to get out at Oxford I shivered in my dusty seat and dreamed of the stately, civilized journey from Montreal to Toronto, and when a row broke out between the ticket collector and a passenger opposite, I closed my eyes and thought of François.

As it happened, I wasn't going all the way to Toronto on the train. I was getting out at Belleville, and here we were, and there was my friend Janet on the platform. Platform is not quite the right word; strictly speaking, there is no platform – stations are divided up into tracks and not-tracks. The train stopped. I dragged my suitcase to the vestibule at the end of the car, where the car attendant was waiting to let us out. Which he did. He took a key and *unlocked the door*, unfolded a set of steps down to ground level and lifted out our luggage; wished us each a good afternoon, beaming farewell. The other passengers seemed to take this for granted, as he turned to assist a wave of oncoming grannies.

Still reeling slightly with surprise I picked up the suitcase and went down the "platform" to meet Janet.

I was out of French Canada. I could go back to speaking nothing but English again; in a way I was almost sorry. But now I was in Prince Edward County, Ontario, on my way to see Bird House City at Picton.

Prince Edward County: it had a familiar ring. Off the coast of Nova Scotia is Canada's smallest province, Prince Edward Island, named, as you might guess, after the Duke of Kent, the frisky martinet of Halifax. Prince Edward County is also named after him. (There are vast tracts of Canada named after Queen Victoria's relatives – look at Alberta. Regina, capital of Saskatchewan, is named after Victoria herself; *regina* being the Latin word for Queen. It is perhaps a happier name than the one the Indians gave it: Pile-of-Bones.)

Edward didn't actually have anything to do with his county, but in the last year that he was in Canada

he served as the commander-in-chief of all British
forces in North America. As Nova Scotia hangs out
into the Atlantic like a lobster, so Prince Edward
County hangs out into Lake Ontario. It doesn't look
like a lobster, exactly, but in its outline there is a
suggestion of snapping pincers.

The history of Prince Edward County goes all the
way back to the American War of Independence, in
1776. We still retain rather patchy notions of the
American War of Independence: the Boston Tea
Party, the Sons of Liberty, the Minutemen, George
Washington, and Paul Revere galloping through the
night crying "The British are coming! The British are
coming!" The overall impression is of the entire
colony rising up in wrath at the unjust taxation levied
by the Government of George III and driving out the
Redcoats sent to repress them. Well, yes and no.

For a start there were, in those days, only thirteen
states, strung along the eastern seaboard. The West
had not yet been opened up. Although the majority
of the colonists were in favour of an end to British rule
a great many were not; the Revolution was as much a
civil war as a rebellion. Communities, neighbour-
hoods, families, found themselves at odds, and when
the war was won the Loyalists, those who had wished
to remain British, were regarded as little better than
traitors. They could not stay, they did not wish to stay,
and they were driven out. There was only one
direction in which to flee and that was north, over the
border and into Canada. The war ended in 1781.
Between April '83 and August '94, thousands of
Loyalist refugees crossed over from the country

which, a few years later, was to become the United States of America.

George III was still king. He promised to do right by those North American colonists who had remained loyal to the Crown, and land was granted to them. New communities began to establish themselves. The Loyalists, driven from their homes and barred from becoming citizens of the new United States, became Canadians instead.

The Revolution had visited on them all the things that they had originally left Britain to escape; repression, persecution, fear. Now they had to start again. They wanted to be at peace and, nearly two hundred years later, it still shows. Prince Edward County, that almost-island, is a quiet, rural, enclosed place, attached to the rest of Ontario by an isthmus, now cloven by the Murray Canal, and by a bridge south of Belleville – where I'd got off the train – over which runs the road to Picton.

Bird House City lies on a gentle slope above a valley near the town. Further down the hillside is the Whattam Memorial Walkway, property of the local undertakers, famous for advertising their premises succinctly as the Whattam Fun. Home. What a way to go – almost as optimistic as the Wing On Funeral Directors in Toronto, a cheerful Chinese enterprise which featured on its sign blond curly-haired cherubs with little wings but no bodies, an anatomy more commonly associated with harpies.

I had come a long way to see Bird House City. It was a lovely, melancholy place, the life's work of Doug Harnes, whose delight it was to make bird houses. It has to be said that the North American bird house is no mere nesting box on a pole. Many of them are multi-storey, beautifully designed, but I never saw any to compete with Doug's creations.

Someone had helpfully provided a kind of map to the museum – which is what it is – by putting up a hoarding near the gate, showing the layout. Every single bird house was marked and identified by a number, but as there was no clue as to what the numbers represented it was impossible to discover what some of the houses were meant to be. The horse was clearly a horse, but others were scale models of real buildings.

The hillside was silent in the mild, sunless afternoon, as I sat drawing the bird houses. There was a feeling of decline, of things coming to an end. The bird houses were certainly coming to an end. Their

"Bird-House City" Picton, Prince Edward County

paint was peeling, fading; some were crumbling, others had fallen away entirely and only the poles remained to mark where they had stood. It seemed sad that something as eccentric, affectionate, cherishable, should be allowed to disintegrate, although later on, when I saw totem poles on Vancouver Island, I remembered the bird houses of Picton and thought that perhaps it was right to let them go.

On the way to Janet's house we drove through an Indian reserve and called in at the shop. There were two to choose from, right next to each other. Between them stood totem poles uneasily distempered in pastel shades, and one of the shops had two cut-out warriors, life size, dancing at the door. We patronized the other, which displayed a large sign outside advertising the attractions of THE ORIGINAL MARACLE MOHAWK CENTRE GIFT SHOP (the Maracles being an important local family). These included Geronimo's picture, signed by his great-granddaughter, which is strange, as Geronimo was famously an Apache chief, and, even more strangely, Tonto's nephew Talking Earth's Clayface Sculpture. I thought I'd work that one out when I saw it, but although I walked all round the store I didn't manage to identify it. I'd assumed it would be hard to miss.

There were no Mohawks serving in the store. Janet thought that probably they were away demonstrating on behalf of the Warriors at the Oka seige which, although now entering what looked like its final phase, was by no means over. The gifts were a mélange of schlock, kitsch and the genuinely beautiful, unlike the work I'd seen in Indian galleries in Quebec, which was all beautiful and all expensive. The message seemed to be: If you cannot tell the difference between art and rubbish you deserve to end up with the rubbish. On a wall hung amazing, intricately woven masks, rather reminiscent of our corn dollies, made to celebrate harvest, although ours are usually woven of wheat straw and these were of maize husks; maize, sweet corn, Indian corn.

The myth of a cereal crop being a god-king, slain, buried and rising from the dead, is common to many cultures, the Ancient Greeks, the Egyptians, the Gonds of India. The English have their song about John Barleycorn. In Longfellow's famous and mono-tonous poem, Hiawatha, to save his people from famine, wrestles with and kills the young man Mondamin, from whose buried body rise the new shoots of Indian corn. Hiawatha, outside of the poem, was a real and powerful chief of the Onondaga nation.

Janet's farmhouse stands near the water's edge overlooking a little bay that lies at the end of the garden. In front are fields. Trees nod over the house and tap at windows. We sat round the stove in the kitchen as darkness fell, darkness and the silence of deep countryside. It was the time for hurricane lamps to be lit; would we carry candles up to bed? No.

That evening we watched a video. Janet showed me her collection and asked what I would like to see. As far as I could tell, there was no choice; it had to be *Rose Marie*. It would have been a seriously missed opportunity to watch anything else, here in Canada.

Rose Marie is a musical comedy (more music than comedy but not much more) set in Canada; Canada, that is, as seen from Hollywood in 1936.

It stars Jeanette Macdonald and Nelson Eddy, a formidable pair who were known, in their day, as the Iron Butterfly and the Singing Capon. I had always felt that the capon bit was unkind, as indeed it is, since a capon is a castrated cockerel, but after about ten minutes I could see the resemblance. He reminded me of someone – or something – no, not a capon, but I couldn't quite recall what.

We watched it because *Rose Marie* is the story of an opera singer and a Mountie. Now, just about every country in the world produces opera singers, but only Canada has the Mounties, the North West Mounted Police. One of the most enduring images of Canada is the Mountie, with his blue breeches, red coat, Boy Scout hat and, of course, a horse. In real life the North West Mounted Police, now the Royal Canadian Mounted Police, are mounted in cars while working, but where Britain sends out a squad of guardsmen in bearskins to perform ceremonial duties, Canada sends the RCMP, in all their gear. Mounties, like Château Frontenac, appear on postcards, place mats, tea towels and – key-rings. When I arrived in Toronto I was given a key-ring with a little plastic Mountie dangling from it. I don't normally travel with a St Christopher, but I'd brought my Mountie along on the trip; though more for company than good luck. A familiar face is consoling when you travel alone.

The plot of *Rose Marie* is not complicated. *She*

is the opera singer whose no-good brother has murdered a Mountie while on the run. She flies north to find him. You can tell it's the north. There are a lot of rugged chaps milling about. *He* is a Mountie (not the one who was murdered) and it is his duty to arrest the no-good brother. He grits his teeth – a position they remain in for much of the movie. The Mounties, remember, Always Get Their Man. By strange coincidence He meets Her. He pitches the woo. They sing. She rebuffs him. They sing some more. He takes her out in a canoe, he sings, he hugs and kisses her, he continues, at intervals, to pursue the no-good brother and *he never takes his hat off.* Once it falls off but, swift as a man applying a tourniquet to a wounded limb, he claps it on again. Janet and I were horridly fascinated by the hat. We were fairly sure that no cop would set out on a manhunt through the mountains wearing a hat roughly the size of a small umbrella, but there was more to it than that. In the end we came to the conclusion that the problem was not the hat itself but the shape of Eddy's head. The hat was round. The head was square. No wonder the two remained so firmly jammed together.

To describe Eddy's acting as wooden is an affront to trees. Sudden movements, his own, seemed to confuse him, and when he moved he moved all of a piece like – like – like my key-ring! At last I knew what he reminded me of. I fetched the key-ring from my suitcase. It was Nelson Eddy to the life, hanging from a hook embedded in the apex of the hat. Even the acting style was similiar.

After this I developed a deep affection for Nelson Eddy and hung him from the zip of my document case that I carried everywhere, containing maps and sketch-books. I decided too that I must find out more about the North West Mounted Police since the facts, as set forth in *Rose Marie*, seemed to be unreliable.

The lowest point of the movie is the Indian Corn Dance. We watched it slack-jawed; it is possibly the most condescending crud ever to appear on celluloid. The "corn" part of the title was accurate enough, though.

They make cheese in Prince Edward County. You can buy it in England, in supermarkets, good, firm, Canadian cheddar. Once there were many cheese factories around Picton, but now they have all been bought up by big conglomerates, and only one is left, Black Mills Cheese Factory, where you can not only buy cheese and bags of wonderful golden curds that squeak when you bite them, but through a little glass window you can watch the cheese being made ... by real people ... with their *hands*.

Canadian cheese is excellent, and without it we would never have been able to enjoy the finest work of James McIntyre, the celebrated Cheese Poet of Ontario.

McIntyre was a Scot who came to Ontario, then Upper Canada, in the early nineteenth century, and much of his verse is a history of his experiences as an immigrant, but he found his true vocation in writing about cheese. His most famous and memorable work celebrates a cheese weighing seven thousand pounds, made by the dairies of Ingersoll, Ontario, to advertise the excellence of their product. It was entitled, "Ode on the Mammoth Cheese".

> We have seen thee, queen of cheese
> Lying quietly at your ease,
> Gently fanned by many a breeze,
> Thy fair form no flies dare seize.
>
> All gaily dressed soon you'll go
> To the great Provincial show,
> To be admired by many a beau
> In the city of Toronto.

It takes a poet to rhyme go, show and beau with Toronto, whose inhabitants call it T'ranna. But greater glories yet awaited the cheese.

> May you not receive a scar as
> We have heard that Mr Harris
> Intends to send you off as far as
> The great world's show at Paris.

McIntyre was eager to spread the word on the proper approach to cheese-making:

> Our muse it doth refuse to sing
> Of cheese made in the early spring,
> The quality is often vile
> Of cheese that is made in April.

He was quite good on the subject of the Great Lakes, too:

Other lakes seem inferior
In size to great Superior.

You can't argue with that.

Lake Superior is also the highest of the Great Lakes (in altitude, not just looking at it on a map, where it seems to be at the top) and the deepest. But it is the shallow lakes that are the most dangerous, when strong winds blow. Imagine you are carrying a bowl of water. It is shallow but full, and heavy. No matter how carefully you handle it, how steadily you hold it, the water inside develops its own momentum. It begins to swing, it begins to slop over the rim. Nothing you can do will quieten it. That is what happens on the Lakes, when the wind blows and the water begins to move, millions of tons of water, inexorably surging.

Next morning we walked on the shores of the bay, along little sandy coves and beaches. The bay is silting up. Tree-cutting and agriculture have loosened the topsoil. On the far side of the county is Soup Harbour, the inspired name of a bay where a ship once sank, loaded with dried peas. Don't you wish you could have seen it?

Prince Edward's is a county of fences: snake fences and stump fences. As the dry stone walls of England are built without mortar, so the fences of Ontario were made without iron; no nails, no wire. They aren't made that way anymore. The snake fence

zigzags, holding itself together with its own weight.
McIntyre again:

> Though it was crooked as a snake,
> And zig-zag style did not awake,
> He thought it was a thing of beauty,
> Yet in its day it did its duty.

Unfortunately the one I saw had been repaired with
wire. There is no way of repairing a stump fence, but
mainly there is no need to. They are made of whole
tree stumps, rooted out and tipped over, the great
groping tangle of roots forming a natural barrier.
Stump fences are *lastiest*, as they say locally. They last
the longest. Lastiest.

In Picton itself I visited an antique shop. The
antiques were not Chippendale chairs, Sheraton
commodes, ormolu clocks, Bristol glass. They were
ordinary, everyday things that spoke of a society
where everything was treasured, kept; nothing
thrown away until it was beyond repair. I've always
wondered at the Canadians' skill in not breaking tea
cups. In Canada you can buy lovely Victorian cups
and saucers anywhere. In England you can usually
buy only the saucers. Go and look in any Oxfam shop
if you don't believe me. I had bought a cup and
saucer at the flea market in Montreal. I was tempted
to buy half a dozen more in Picton, but what caught
my eye, in Montreal and Picton, was the number of
old milk bottles for sale.

Yes, I smiled too, the first time I saw a sign urging
the public to invest in old milk bottles, as it were,

while stocks lasted. However, these were not just any old milk bottles. They were the kind that I remember from very early childhood in London, shaped rather like the cooling towers on power stations, with wide tops, into which slotted cardboard caps, a couple of inches across. I hadn't seen one of those for more than forty years. I remembered the greatest of treats, licking the cream off the underside of the cardboard cap and I felt very ancient. It's always disconcerting to see something that you have used yourself in a museum or antique shop.

We were driving to meet some friends for dinner, a mere hundred miles away. Afterwards I was going to catch the stopping train back to Toronto, but Janet was driving home again, another hundred miles ... so what's a hundred miles in a country three thousand miles across? All the road signs are in kilometres, which makes everything seem much further off, anyway.

The last place we stopped at in Prince Edward County was a shop that sold nice things; there was really no other way to describe it. It wasn't a gift shop, a tourist trap; it just sold nice things that you might like to use around the house. On the counter stood a bowl of polished red apples. "Have some," said the owner, as we paid for our purchases, so we took one each. That was my abiding memory of Prince Edward County, and somehow summed it up; that act of unthinking courtesy that comes as second nature.

It is something I associate with Canada anyway. The British writer Jan Morris called it "public kindness", but you can't generalize about twenty-six million people, especially in a country so little given to telling the rest of the world how wonderful it is.

That unusual prime minister William Lyon Mackenzie King once said, "... if some countries have too much history, we have too much geography." Said Janet, as we drove along, "You will never understand Canada or Canadians unless you realize that the Arctic is part of us; the awareness of its being there. Not of *owning* it, but the feeling that this otherness is ours."

This feeling is perhaps due to the fact that the majority of Canadians live on the bottom line, as you might say, along the forty-ninth parallel, the border with the United States; in cities, with advanced transport, reliable communications, all mod cons, in fact, and yet have access to infinity. It is a feeling perhaps shared with Swedes, Norwegians, Russians – who no doubt take it for granted. Canadians don't seem to take anything for granted, their land or themselves; always the question, Who are we? Why are we here?

"The true Canadian," said Janet, "was William Lyon Mackenzie King, who looked like your average corporate lawyer (he certainly did in the Musée de Cire in Quebec) yet ruled this country with a crystal ball and the help of his mother, whose spirit, he thought, inhabited the body of his pet terrier, Pat. He built fake ruins at Ottawa and, like William Ewart Gladstone, the great English Victorian premier, went out into the streets at night to redeem prostitutes. What went on in his *head*?" Janet mused.

They take nothing for granted. Canada has the

world's largest sources of fresh water and cannot quite get over its luck. "If this country ever went to war with the United States," David once said to me, in Toronto, "it would be over water, not oil."

It is also bigger than the United States, a fact which they delight in retailing to US citizens. I checked this out and it is true; 9,970,610 km^2 against 9,372,614 km^2. Too much geography...

Becoming a naturalized Canadian is a serious yet festive business. You take the kids out of school for the day, the ceremony is performed with tears in the eyes. You swear allegiance to the Queen, which tends to stick in the craw of US citizens who are passing over. A curious thought struck me.

"Do you have to do that even if you're British already?"

Apparently, yes.

"What is it about Canada?" a friend asked me, when I got home. "What's the attraction?"

I thought about this, remembering something else that David had said. "What holds us together? This is an artificial country, like the United States. All that holds the US together is its rampant jingoism, and we've never had that."

He wasn't the first to think this. In 1892, Archibald Lampman wrote:

> We cannot be patriotic as the Englishman is patriotic. Born and bred in an old and famous land covered with the monuments and remnants of a romantic history ... the Englishman indeed were not at the level of humanity if he had not

patriotism. With us it is very different. We have no magnificent race history behind us ... we are indeed only the scattered and intractable materials of which a nation may be made ... our patriotism is founded upon duty and the sense of honour. But it is none the less real... Even among our neighbours of the United States, with the memory of some heroic national experiences behind them, the old-fashioned fiery and affectionate love of native land is not fully developed, as the exaggerated gasconading exhibition of it in their public press distinctly shows.

That's the attraction; the size, the grandeur, the pioneering heroism, the adventure, without the chest-thumping, without the violence. There is no pride in a bloody history, all measures having been taken to avoid a bloody history; no shoot-outs at the OK Corral or at the Little Big Horn, no lynch mobs, cattle rustlers, no insistence on the right to bear arms and blow out the brains of your fellow citizens.

The only guns I had ever heard in Canada had been at the lakeside that very morning, loosing off at wild fowl; legitimate, but not much admired.

Chapter Six

They say of Calgary that it looks as if it had just been unpacked. The first time I saw it, on a golden autumn evening, hot-air balloons were floating over the downtown core which seemed nothing more than misty silhouettes. Today the sun shone and the skyscrapers were glossy, just like things that had been newly taken from a box and left standing around while someone decided where to put them.

Chris and Jean live in the suburbs, beyond the University. Chris is an old friend and I've been writing to that address for years. Now I saw it, a house in a quiet cul-de-sac, English-looking but not *quite* English, in that perplexing way of houses in countries like Canada and Australia, that were first colonized by the British. How is it that you know immediately that this is *not* England? It isn't solely the absence of litter.

An arctic hare spends his white winters under a bush in the garden. Down the road is Varsity Acres, the common with a pond, where people go to hear the frogs sing in springtime, just as they do at Julie's Pond in Halifax.

There were no frogs now. It was late September,

officially fall, but tomorrow it might be winter. With the Rockies shouldering over the horizon you tend to assume that Calgary, out on the prairie, is low-lying. In fact it is 1,049 metres above sea level. It could be said that Calgary, like Montreal, has two seasons; in this case, winter and not winter. The growing season lasts three months. Those petunias glowing in a tub by Chris's front door could be blackened rags tomorrow morning.

That evening the seige of the Kanesatake reserve at Oka came to an end in violence and confusion. Next morning the radio news and the papers carried reports of the final moments. The Mohawks – Warriors, women, children – and ten Canadian journalists, had left the treatment centre after a ritual fire and tobacco ceremony. The troops, taken unawares by the sudden mass exodus, scuffled with the Mohawks, and fighting broke out. Helicopters hovered overhead and troops were ordered to fix bayonets. Women and children were mishandled.

The radio reporter being interviewed was exhausted; worried about a child who had been the subject of an article he had written – what had become of her? He admitted that he had entered the reserve biased and ready to consider the Mohawk Warriors as mindless thugs. Now, he said, maybe one or two were mindless thugs, but he had nothing but respect for most of them.

What would happen next was unclear. "These people in our minds are heroes," said an Oneida chief who had handled negotiations on behalf of the

Warriors. "They will be revered as a people who have created a very positive change in the relationship between aboriginal peoples and governments."

Lawrence Cortoreille, Alberta Vice-Chief to the Assembly of First Nations, said that if native people had learned a lot from Oka, the government had learned more.

The prime minister, as prime ministers will, hailed the surrender, as he called it, as a victory for "firmness, patience and concern for human life".

The reporter wanted only beer, sleep and cigarettes, but at least he'd got his story out. While I was in Quebec it had become clear that one of the most outrageous aspects of the whole affair was that the military were effectively censoring all news reports. The journalists who had left the treatment centre on Wednesday night had been holed up there with the Mohawks, unable to communicate with the outside world, their phone lines cut.

I couldn't help comparing the situation to the Troubles in Northern Ireland, where festering discontent, initially treated with indifference by successive governments, finally erupted, but for a long while went underestimated. Chris thought not. I hoped not, and I hoped that another Albertan Indian, Richard Davis, was right when he said, "Things are never going back to the way they were before."

A few days later, someone talking about Oka said to me, "I don't know how they've waited so long. They've been so *patient*."

* * *

One of the reasons I'd come to Calgary, apart from wanting to see Chris and Jean, was to revisit an old acquaintance out at Banff. I had a particular urge to do this because the old acquaintance was so very peculiar that I had never yet met a Canadian who had heard of her, much less met her. I had to go back to make sure that I really had seen ... what I thought I'd seen.

In 1885 a sulphur spring was discovered in the Rockies, and the following year the CPR built the first of its hotels at Banff Springs. The original building was of wood; nowadays the Banff Springs Hotel is a stone castle, a slightly flatter version of Château Frontenac, and with the same green copper roofs. All around it loom mountains, coniferous forests; cataracts fall from Cascade Mountain. Somehow the Banff Springs Hotel is not dwarfed by the grandeur of the scenery. You cannot dwarf a CPR hotel.

It was a fine bright day. The sun shone as we left Calgary, driving west on the switchback of the Trans-Canada Highway towards the mountains. Soon after we left town we saw, assembled on a slight rise a little way from the road, a great company of men on horseback, an unsettling sight. It was the wrong time of year for the famous Calgary Stampede, a ten-day rodeo held in July. I wondered if they could be film extras, but they had none of that near-hysterical boredom that hangs over film sets. Chris suggested nervously that they might be Indians ... massing. (The following day we learned that it was a charity cattle drive – the prairie version of a sponsored walk.)

As soon as we reached Banff we headed straight for the Indian Trading Post, where I was to make my rendezvous – if I hadn't been dreaming that first time, back in 1986. It was all just as I remembered it, the plastic wampum key rings, the fibreglass reproductions of Inuit sculpture. There were the postcards: long shots of Mounted Policemen, close-ups of mountain goats – possibly the world's most gormless-looking creatures – and bison, aka buffalo, possibly the world's most depressed-looking animal – with reason. Beyond the tourist trap lay the back room; nothing had changed. On the wall were the stuffed heads of buffalo and elk; there were the stacks of hides, the heaps of furs, and there, at the back, just where I saw her last, was my old friend, my dear old, wizened old, mummified friend, inexplicably marooned in the mountains – the Mermaid of Banff.

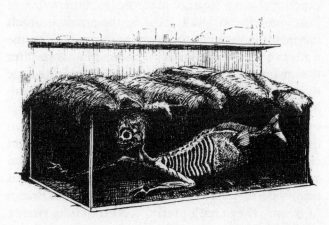

The Mermaid of Banff

The Mermaid of Banff lives in a glass case which stands on the floor, partially obscured by a pile of hides, in a dark corner. The owners of the Indian Trading Post do not care to draw attention to it. Nobody notices it. Nobody was noticing it as I sat down on the floor to draw it. After that, people, courteously stepping round me, paused to see what I was sketching. Suddenly the Mermaid was receiving more attention than it normally attracts in a year, I would guess. Every now and again a girlish voice overhead would cry, "Oh – *gross!*"

A sticker on the glass case which houses it has that weary, slightly defensive tone discernible in the sign on The Wave in Halifax. THIS, it said, IS ALL WE KNOW ABOUT THIS MAMMAL. So people do notice it sometimes and ask unanswerable questions. I'm not sure that I'd mention mammals, if I were the Indian Trading Post. Beside the sign is an ancient newspaper clipping about a creature that rose from the waters of Lake Superior in 1824. That is, the article is about mermaids in general; the creature that rose from the waters of Lake Superior is mentioned in passing. An unconvincing sketch shows something rearing out of the water and waving, in a yoo-hoo sort of fashion. None of this explains the Mermaid herself.

The explanation could be simple. Sailors used to find that your mermaid was a nice little earner and cobble them together from the top half of a monkey and the rear end of a fish, for sale to credulous landlubbers. I have seen examples in the British Museum. They aren't pretty – you couldn't imagine one luring mariners to their doom – but they are

quite dainty. There is nothing dainty about this thing.
For a start it is over a metre long, and although the
back part is definitely a fish, the front doesn't look
quite like a monkey. Its blackened leathery skin bears
tufts of fur, its clawing fingers are webbed. No
monkey ever had so many teeth. And what is it doing
here in the Rocky Mountains, five hundred miles
from the sea?

I finished my drawing and left reluctantly. I shall
return. I bought some postcards of it which, in a way,
are even more grisly than the real thing, for to be
photographed the Mermaid was taken out of its
cabinet and posed in the sunshine. Certain distressing
details show up more clearly. Even the fishy end bears
fur. Dear God ... *how* many ribs has it got...? I recalled
the item in the *Weekly World News* about the
mermaid's skeleton found in a shark's stomach. I
thought of Ross Jobe of Saulte Ste Marie, Ontario,
who once created a fur-bearing trout (I have seen it)
which, he said, lived in the icy waters of Lake
Superior. If you ask me, there's no accounting for
what comes out of the waters of Lake Superior. It's a
nice little thing, wearing a sort of fish-shaped fur
mitten, but it doesn't come anywhere near to solving
the mystery of the Mermaid of Banff.

I had left England in the parched grip of a drought.
That morning I had been shaken to see Chris,
wanting a drink, running the tap prodigally until the
water was really cold. Part of the shock was due to the
thought of drinking anything that has come straight
out of the tap (strange things come out of Oxford
taps) but it was also the memory of my summer spent

lugging bath water to the end of the garden to revive wilting plants. So much water, washing heedlessly down the plug hole. I thought of it again as we stood in the street in Banff, looking at the face of Cascade Mountain. I should have thought it a fanciful name if I hadn't seen it before, when icy cataracts leaped from the summit. Today a single trickle ran down. Dry watercourses veined the surface of the rock. What was missing was snow, snow on the summit to feed the falls.

Banff lies at the feet of three peaks, Cascade, Rundle and Sulphur mountains. Chris suggested that we took the gondola to the top of Sulphur Mountain. This sounded as likely as walking round Venice on snowshoes, but the gondola is a car on the lift to the summit. At ground level you can see why they are called the *Rocky* Mountains. Rock is the first word that comes to mind; great grey pyramids of rock, slabby planes, jackknife angles forced massively from the earth. Up among the summits they seem to float like ice floes, peak after peak after peak, on and on into the blue northern distance. Each mountain wore its own little white cap of cloud, but there was no snow, anywhere.

Sulphur Mountain is clad in trees, conical, coniferous.

"What are they?" I asked Chris, feeling that I ought to know.

"Douglas fir," he said, and then I remembered: I did know. We looked at the trees and simultaneously recalled a song that we had both learned long ago.

As I sat down one evening
Within a small café,
A forty-year-old waitress
To me these words did say:

"I see you are a logger
And not a common bum,
For no one but a logger
Stirs his coffee with his thumb.

"My lover was a logger,
There's none like him today;
If you poured whiskey on it,
He'd eat a bale of hay.

"He never shaved the whiskers
From off his horny hide,
But he drove 'em in with a hammer
And bit 'em off inside.

"My logger came to see me
On one freezing day,
He held me in a fond embrace
That broke three vertebrae.

"He kissed me when we parted
So hard he broke my jaw;
I could not speak to tell him
He'd forgot his mackinaw.

"I saw my logger lover
  Sauntering through the snow
  A-going gaily homeward
  At forty-eight below.

"The weather tried to freeze him,
  It tried its level best.
  At one hundred degrees below zero
  He buttoned up his vest.

"It froze clear through to China,
  It froze to the stars above,
  At one thousand degrees below zero
  It froze my logger love.

"They tried in vain to thaw him,
  And if you'll believe me, sir,
  They sectioned him into axe-blades
  To chop the Douglas fir.

"And so I lost my lover
  And to this café I come.
  And here I wait till someone
  Stirs his coffee with his thumb."

There wasn't time to visit Thunder Mountain, a little (comparatively) furry tump that stands behind the Banff Springs Hotel, to see the hoodoos – wind-sculpted columns of softer rock that reminded me of the howling statues in Samuel Butler's novel *Erewhon*. And there was no time to search again for the frozen lake into which the hot spring runs. In thick frost I once saw summer flowers blooming along the sides of the warm streamlet as it ran down the mountainside. Where it flowed into the lake tropical fish swarmed in the water. Years ago, some enquiring-minded youth emptied his aquarium into this warm stream to see what would happen. What happened was that the fish loved it. Now you can walk out over the lake on a wooden platform. All around, the lake is skinned with ice, but in the warm water the little tropical Pacific fish swim to and fro. A stern notice warns any other airhead against trying the same thing, possibly to avoid upsetting the delicate ecological balance, possibly in case someone experiments with a tankful of piranha fish.

That night, back in Calgary, we had the threatened frost, four degrees below. It warmed up quickly enough next morning, but suddenly, all the leaves had gone from Calgary's thousands of trees. They stand all over the city, identical in size, identical in species, and when one goes, they all go.

Calgary's CPR hotel, the Palliser, is built right over the railway which ran from Banff, through the Kicking Horse Pass. The railway is still there. The trains no longer run; they have been diverted through the Yellowhead Pass, a cheaper route and further north. Chris told of weeping crowds who gathered to watch the last train pull out, and of people's deep resentment that the government would not let the train make a symbolic stop where the last spike had been driven in when the railway was built. We went into the Palliser for lunch, and also to admire the grand lobby where, in wilder times, persons celebrating the Calgary Stampede once rode their horses. Since then the Queen has dropped in and the wooden columns have been painstakingly painted to resemble marble. We hoped that Her Majesty had noticed.

The Palliser is in the downtown core, the unpacked part of Calgary. A little further along the road, where the skyscrapers come to a sudden stop, stands Fort Calgary, not the heart of the city, which has grown away from it, but the seed from which it sprang. It lies at the place where the Elbow river runs into the Bow, at an extraordinarily precise right angle that looks as if it were man-made. Not so; there was nothing at Calgary before the arrival of a detachment of mounted riflemen in 1875. This was one of the very first outposts established when Canada began to expand westward.

The Fort is small, a square that you can walk around in a few minutes. Where the stockade stood, posts have been driven into the earth so that now you can see the layout. The Union Jack flies over it, not the Maple Leaf. And it was not an army fort. I had assumed it must have been, thinking of the US Cavalry, Fort Sumner, Fort Laramie, and I might have gone on thinking it, after seeing the photographs on display, of the original garrison. In one of these the men are on parade, and they look exactly like a file of British soldiers, drawn up to attention; but they were not ... quite. Here, at last, I discovered the facts behind the postcards, the key-ring, and Nelson Eddy.

For these men were the North West Mounted

Police. How could they be? Where, for a start, was the hat? These guys were not Nelson Eddy. They were your average nineteenth-century cavalrymen, the types who, twenty years earlier, had charged with the Light Brigade at Balaclava.

In a sense they were just that. When Canada began to look westward, in the latter half of the last century, it saw and learned an important lesson from the events that were taking place south of the border; the wars fought by the Americans with the Plains Indians. Canada was still a relatively small country and the prime minister, Sir John Macdonald, knew that it could not afford Indian wars on the scale experienced in the United States. There would be no Fort Fetterman massacre, no Battle of the Little Big Horn, no Wounded Knee atrocity as the Canadians went west.

There was already unwelcome activity; uprisings among the French settlers who were there in advance of the British, and illicit whiskey salesmen from Montana causing havoc among the native people who were entirely unaccustomed to alcohol, stationing themselves at places with such resounding names as Fort Whoop-Up. Indians poisoned on alcohol were not whooping it up in the genial fashion the name suggests. Macdonald's plan was that the law should establish itself in the western territories before the settlers arrived, and it must be *one* law, the same for French and British, Indians and whites, honestly and impartially enforced.

The solution he came up with was to send out a paramilitary force which would act as policemen rather than as soldiers. Originally they were to have been the North West Mounted Rifles, organized along the lines of the British cavalry – such as the Light Brigade – but a tactful inspiration made him change the name at the last moment. They were to be known as the North West Mounted Police, which they remained until the 1920s.

It was not to be a large force, but it was to be a highly conspicuous one, hence the red coats. Anyone (and Sir John had, particularly, encroaching Americans in mind) could see a red coat from a very long way off in that open, featureless terrain, and so, in the summer of 1874, the first force rode west into what was to become Alberta. There were just over three hundred of them (even at its peak the force never grew above a thousand) who established themselves at Fort McLeod, and in the following year a detachment of thirty-five was sent to establish a new fort at the confluence of the Bow and Elbow rivers.

The Long March from the east had been gruelling. Now they were on their own. They had to be self-sufficient. Among the original force had been two surgeons and one vet. They had to grow or hunt for their own food, raise hay for the all-important horses. Standing in Fort Calgary and facing away from the skyscrapers it was almost possible to imagine them, thirty-five men in that immense and lonely landscape, the Rockies to the west and on the other three sides, beyond the rivers, nothing. Those trees that grow in Calgary were planted by the city itself. They were not there before.

Colonel James McLeod named the fort after his birthplace in Scotland. Now it is one of the largest cities in Canada. The Mounties continued to flourish, too, in spite of constant suggestions that they should be disbanded, as new towns and cities established their own police forces. Gradually their appearance changed. The British army drill and organization remained, but the men adopted American saddles, gear and, of course, the hat, although it is worn now only on ceremonial occasions, like the red coat, that highly visible symbol of law and security in a land which might otherwise have been as violent as the American West.

One notable testimonial to their reputation was the action of the Dakota chief, Sitting Bull, after the Battle of the Little Big Horn. Knowing that the Indians' devastating victory could do them no good in the long run he led his people over the border into Canada, trusting, correctly, that Queen Victoria's Mounted Police would not betray them although her government abandoned them.

All the while we were at the fort we could see aircraft rising above us as they took off from the north of the city. Later that afternoon, when I too was aboard a DC9, flying to Vancouver, I remembered to look down as we banked over the city. There, below, in the angle of the two rivers, lay little Fort Calgary. I mentally blotted out the skyscrapers, the tower, the suburbs, the stadiums, the University, and saw the outpost as it must once have been, alone in all that prairie, flying the Union Jack that flies over it now, manned by those few red-coated policemen sent out to make the new Canada safe. And they did. And they must have felt as if they were at the end of the world.

Chapter Seven

The Trans-Canada Highway unrolled below. What I was hoping for was that the sky should remain clear, as clear as it had been yesterday when we stood on Sulphur Mountain looking up at the vapour trails, so that when the plane passed over Banff I should have one last sight of Sulphur Mountain, Cascade Mountain and Mount Rundle. But as we left the prairie behind, the first clouds were massing around the first of the mountains. There was an occasional glimpse of a peak or a rock-face, but soon it was all cloud. I did not see when we passed into British Columbia.

BC, the province that has everything. "When Quebec breaks up the nation," said Chris, among others, "BC will join the United States."

The United States would be delighted to include British Columbia; will welcome it with open arms for its scenery, sports facilities, its oil and gas and water; water again.

Newfoundland would like to join the US too, he said, but would the US want a bunch of dirt-poor fishermen?

This seems to be the usual way of describing Newfoundlanders; Newfies. I remembered hearing it once before, during a discussion on seal hunting. The clubbing of baby seals to make fur coats caused revulsion in Europe, but – "It was the chance for a few dirt-poor fishermen to make a few bucks once a year," said David, on that occasion. I hadn't visited Newfoundland for the same reason that I wasn't visiting the Northern Territories; I didn't feel it was a place I wanted to go and gawp at, a stranger dropping in and dropping out again, but I had heard people talk of picturesque Newfoundland villages where the healthy fresh air came through cracks in the walls. I've been poor, but never dirt poor. The thought of clubbing anything to death makes me cringe, it hurts physically even to think about it. But I am not dirt poor.

British Columbia agreed to join the Canadian confederation in 1871, after the government had agreed to link it to the rest of the country with the Canadian Pacific Railway. Newfoundland was the last province to sign up, and that was not until 1949. So there was BC in the west, with everything, and Newfoundland in the east with nothing, and yet somehow, up till now, Canada has held them together.

In his office Chris had a poster pinned up with a poem on it: "What is a Canadian?" by Miriam Waddington. This, I thought, might be an attempt to address the question that a lot of Canadians seem to be asking themselves a lot of the time, a question that floats to the surface of conversations at dinner. But the poem offered no answers, only more questions.

What is a Canadian
anyway? a mountain, a maple
leaf, a prairie, a Niagara Fall,
a trail beside the Atlantic, a
bilingualism, a scarred mosaic,
a yes-no somehow-or-other maybe –
might-be should-be could-be
glacial shield, grain elevator,
empire daughter imperial order of
man woman child or what?

"Do the English sit around after meals discussing
what it means to be English?" Kathy asked me once.
I said no, at the time, but I've thought harder about
it since. A hundred and fifty years ago, when various
ancestors had just migrated here from Ireland and
Spain, I might have spent a lot more time wondering
what it meant to be English. For people more
recently immigrant the question must be very much
more immediate. Canada is a vast, mainly industrial
and agricultural nation, with a relatively small population of every race and colour, occupying a strip
roughly 4,828 kilometres long and 483 kilometres
deep. And yet: "You can never understand Canada or
Canadians unless you realize that the Arctic is part of
us."

As we came down towards Vancouver the clouds
dispersed and below lay ridge after ridge of mountain
tops, the Coastal Range, hazed in a miraculous indigo
twilight. Such a colour I had never seen in real life –
it looked like a photograph taken through a filter for
a tourist brochure. Someone told me later that it was

probably caused by pollution, which might have accounted for the chemical aspect.

The aircraft flew low over the city, out to sea, turned steeply and descended for a smooth landing at the airport. The first time I came to Vancouver, the first time I came to Canada, we arrived in darkness. The plane landed on one wheel and bounced three times, while the pilot shrieked, "Welcome to beeeeeyootiful Vancouver!" and the passengers broke into ironic applause.

On the concourse I rang my contact, Chuck, yet another Canadian prepared to drop everything at a moment's notice and help a total stranger, and who had found me a hotel. It was on the far side of the city, but all I had to do was take a cab.

I left the airport and found a cab. It was a mini-van and I sat up front, next to the driver. We were destined for each other.

"My name's Mike. What's yours?"

"Jan."

"Hello, Jan."

"Hello, Mike."

"And what brings you to Vancouver?"

"I'm writing a book."

"You're here to publicize it?"

"No, I'm still writing it. It's about Canada."

"I'm looking for a publisher," Mike remarked, and whipped his typescript from under the dashboard. He explained that it was an allegory based on the city council's attitude towards speeding fines as a useful source of revenue.

Like our tax on tobacco, the fines are officially

prohibitive but if they dried up there would be a large hole in the budget. The council, said Mike, had no interest at all in stopping people from speeding, just in collecting the fines. So far, so predictable. Then the plot took a more sinister turn.

Many of the traffic cops (RCMP) are Sikhs. The older generation of Sikhs, seeing the younger one allowing itself to become assimilated, had begun agitating to join the RCMP and wear turbans instead of regulation headgear, thus making themselves instantly identifiable, especially to people with a grievance; such as those who had been nicked for speeding.

"Once people were pissed off with the cops," Mike said. "Now they're pissed off with the Pakis."

It was a shock to hear that word used here – I never had before. Sikhs don't come from Pakistan, but in Vancouver, as in England, it is just an insulting term for anyone who is, or looks, Asian. Mike himself could easily have been Asian although he'd told me he was English, born opposite the British Museum. But what is an Englishman? What is a Canadian? Come to that, what is an Asian? In Vancouver it's someone from China or Japan. The people known as Asians in Britain they call East Indians – as opposed to West Indians from the Caribbean. It took a little while to work all this out because if we talk about the East Indies at all, these days, we mean Sumatra, Java or Bali.

Mike's story looked highly entertaining and possibly libellous.

A green copper roof stood out among other high

buildings. "That's got to be a CPR hotel," I said, cleverly. It was; the Hotel Vancouver, last of the railway châteaux, built in 1939.

I was staying at a different hotel, a modern one, overlooking the Burrard Inlet. The television set had thirty-six channels. I tried them all in turn.

Next morning Chuck took me for an inaugural drive round Vancouver before turning me loose on foot. The hotel was in North Vancouver. We drove back to the city centre over Lion's Gate Bridge, and through Stanley Park. The park is severed from the city by Lagoon Drive that sweeps round the shores of Lost Lagoon, where Pauline E. Johnson, the First Nation poet, loved to paddle her canoe. We stopped at a place called Lookout, just off the main road, which gave a view over Siwash Rock, a volcanic plug just offshore with one tree growing out of it; and where there stands a little memorial tablet to Pauline Johnson.

Subsequent research suggests that there may have been a certain amount of window dressing as regards Pauline Johnson. Her father was a Mohawk but her mother was English. She came from near Brantford, Ontario, and retired to Vancouver a few years before she died. One of her books of poetry was called *Flint and Feather* and was not particularly highly thought of. On the other hand she was a popular performer of her work, for which events she wore Indian dress.

It is strange to think of the lagoon ever having been lost. Stanley Park is partly landscaped, but much of it is untouched rain forest. Now the city reaches to the very edge of it. The freeway skirts it. I had walked in Stanley Park before and intended to revisit it. Today though, we were bound for Chinatown, the largest in Canada and snidely known locally as Hongcouver, to view two of its attractions: the Dr Sun Yat Sen Classical Garden, and the shallowest building in the world on Pender Street.

The shallowest building in the world is twenty-nine metres wide and two metres deep, and currently houses Jack Chow's Insurance Store. Back in 1903 a company bought the land to build on, but before they could do so, the city council widened Pender Street. Nothing daunted, the owners went ahead and built on what was left, all six feet of it.

They managed to cheat themselves a little extra space upstairs by building a series of glassed-in verandahs, and downstairs is disorientingly lined with mirrors, which give an illusion not so much of space as of being spaced out.

The Classical Chinese Garden is just down the road. This part of Vancouver does not look like the setting for any kind of a garden, being adjacent to the bus depot, the rail terminus, the sports stadium. The streets are crowded. There are parking lots, business premises, a newspaper office and, in the middle of all this, a long and featureless wall enclosing – well, it is difficult to imagine what might lie inside; a swimming pool, perhaps.

Inside the wall is a public park with a pool (not for swimming in); tranquil, landscaped, Oriental, but inescapably a public park. Within the park lies the

Classical Garden, the emphasis being on the word classical. This is a garden built to rules, a Suzhou garden, which must contain four elements: 1. Pavilions, walkways and terraces from which to look out at; 2. plants; 3. rocks and 4. water. It seems infinite, for every pavilion, bridge and courtyard looks out through windows and doorways to other vistas. In fact it is tiny, but you could spend all day there, day after day, seeking new views. People buy season tickets.

The Water Pavilion, Dr Sun Yat Sen Garden – Vancouver

The garden is named after the man who brought down the last of the Manchu rulers of China and established the Republic, in 1911, of which he was the first president. He lived for a time in Vancouver. It seems strange to walk in the garden that bears his name, this enclosure of peace and contemplation, and to contemplate the chaos and convulsion that have been China ever since.

It is also a wonderful spot for tourist-watching. Chuck was bitter as we stood on a path, gazing down to the milky water that is exactly the colour of jade, and quoted his least favourite rubbernecks. "Why don't they clean the water, Joe?" (Americans) and "It's draughty here, isn't it, why don't they glaze the windows?" (British).

"The Americans," said Chuck, "want America duplicated wherever they go. Near as dammit bring their own houses with them, in campers. Even have satellite dishes on the roof so they can watch genuine American television."

After that I was particularly aware of an English couple, crabby and carping and failing to notice any of the wonders around them. She carried the camera. He issued orders about what was to be photographed, how, when, where, which way the camera should be held, from which angle the picture should be taken. He never stopped, and never stopped to observe the effect he was creating. "Do this, do that, might as well not bother, oh, leave it, come on, over there, step back, oh, get on with it." I wondered why they had laid out good money getting themselves to Canada in order to quarrel in public when they could

have done it for free back in Eastbourne or Worthing.
I longed to shove him into the Pool of Harmonious
Waters, or whatever it was called, as I went past, but
that would have been contrary to the spirit of the
place. If anyone is daft enough to throw coins into
these pools, the jade green waters hide them, though
up at the salmon hatchery at Capilano I noticed that
even the fish tanks were full of loose change.

The next port of call was Grouse Mountain,
ascended, like Sulphur Mountain, by gondola, only
the gondolas here are the size of a bus. On this
occasion the price of the ticket included the entrance
fee to an Experience that was taking place on top of
the mountain. I would have thought that just being
on top of the mountain was enough of an experience
for the view was stupendous, over North Vancouver,
the Burrard Inlet, the city, the Capilano Valley and
away into the atmospheric pollution. To the south a
snow-capped peak hung mysteriously above the
horizon, somewhere down in the United States.

This, however, was only *an* experience, not *the*
Experience. A kind of exhibition centre and cinema
had been built on the summit. On display in the foyer
was a "Transformation Eagle Mask" carved by the
sculptor Robert Davidson. He was also billed to
feature in the Experience which was worryingly
entitled *Soar to the Sky*. We entered the auditorium
and sat down. On either wall hung three television
screens, in front was a triple cinema screen. The lights
went down. The Experience began: voices, music,
panoramas, a dazzling clangour, too loud, too bright.
A local poet intoned. The decibel count rose. Long

John Baldry sang (you won't remember him). Robert Davidson spoke. At once you had to pay attention. Davidson is a Haida Indian from Vancouver Island and he told of his Transformation Mask, recalling an incident in his boyhood when his grandmother pointed overhead to a passing eagle and said, "That's your uncle." Somehow you could believe it. This man took for granted his affinity with other life forms. He was utterly matter of fact, and I wanted to hear more, but he was hopelessly trivialized by the deafening celebration of Beeeeeyootiful Vancouver that swamped him.

Aware of Chuck sitting beside me I wondered how to respond politely, as a foreigner, to all this razzmatazz. OK, we were on the West Coast, but it was the west coast of *Canada* and all this struck me as very un-Canadian, the strident self-advertising, the vaingloriousness, the insensitivity that supposed that this raucous nonsense could in any way enhance the real beauty of the city which was all out there at the foot of the mountain, in clear view.

I needn't have worried about trying to be tactful. Chuck leaned over and muttered, "This is all your fault."

"*Mine?*"

"The British – for exporting Andrew Lloyd Webber."

We staggered out on to the viewing platform to recover and agreed that Robert Davidson had been ill-served. Chuck is a great admirer of Haida art, and a collector. We had visited his house on the way to Grouse Mountain, where he had many examples of

First Nation work, including several frogs. Frogs turn up all over the place in the art of the Haida and Tsimshian people. There was even a Frog Clan, and it was from Chuck that I learned of the ultimate Canadian frog, Phyllidula. Ezra Pound, the odd American poet, wrote a little ode to her:

Phyllidula is scrawny but amorous,
Thus have the gods awarded her,
That in pleasure she receives more
    than she can give;
If she does not count this blessed
Let her change her religion.

Bill Reid, another sculptor with Haida connections, carved a figure of Phyllidula in red cedar, over a metre long. It is called "*The Shape of Frogs to Come*".

West Coast Frog.
"Phyllidula"
by Bill Reid – Vancouver

My last view from Grouse Mountain was down into the Capilano Valley, where a dam spans the river. The water level was very low. Flying from Calgary, before we hit cloud, I'd noticed the low water level in several reservoirs. What had become of the snow?

Chuck and I parted at the seabus terminal, just around the corner from the hotel where I had stayed the night before. For the rest of my time in Vancouver I was going to a guest house on the far side of the city. The seabus is a rather swish ferry, quite unlike the fat little boats at Halifax. On the further shore it docked at the terminal which, with a heliport and a subway station, now lies behind the stately frontage of what was once the main railway station. Down the road is the cradle of Vancouver, the place where it all started, Gastown. Chuck had told me to be sure and visit Gastown, just along Cordova Street and first left, but it was getting late. Gastown could wait till Monday. I set out to walk home across the city.

Vancouver is one of those North American cities built on a grid pattern. Getting home, I reckoned, would be tiring but simple, and I was right. You cannot get lost. From the terminal it was just a matter of right angles, going straight up Seymour, right on Georgia, left on Burrard, and on and on. The road would cross False Creek by the Burrard Bridge. I remembered the Burrard Bridge and I was happy to see it again. Traffic roared over it headachingly, and it takes about ten minutes to walk across, but the view is wonderful.

On the south side of the bridge, consult the map again; at the intersection go straight uphill on

Burrard, over 4th Avenue, Broadway, 9th, 12th. Turn right down 16th, left on to Cypress, right again on to 17th and here was the house. I also, finally, managed to crack the secret of those apparently interminable North American streets with telephone-number addresses. You tend to imagine a road with five thousand houses along it, stretching out across the prairie, perhaps. The truth turned out to be simple and sensible. Where streets are laid out on a grid, it is the *blocks* that are numbered: 900, 1000, 1500. Even if there is only one house on the block and only a dozen on the whole street, it may still be 1020 Acacia Avenue. And number 1020 on any street will be in a straight line with number 1020 on any other street. In the part of Vancouver where I was staying only the avenues running east-west are numbered. The north-south streets have names; round here they are named after trees. Growing confident, I strolled around a little. My block lay betwen Cypress and Maple.

You can't get lost.

It can take a long while to find a pedestrian crossing, though. In the end I pretended to be a wild Montrealer and hurled myself across 16th without even looking for a WALK sign.

I was honour bound to go as far west as I could, so I decided to spend Sunday on Vancouver Island or, rather, in getting to Vancouver Island and back. It's a long journey, beginning at the bus station on Dunsmuir – an hour's walk from my place on 17th. The bus takes you to the terminal at Tsawwassen and from there the ferry crosses the strait of Georgia, tacking between the coastal islands to Swartz Bay.

I started early, the streets were empty; even the Burrard Bridge was quiet. In the city centre I saw my first graffito in the west. *Put on a tie and grovel*, it said, succinctly. Canadian graffiti artists tend to be pithy, make a point and move on. I never saw any really rude remarks, perhaps they get cleaned off too quickly.

When I reached the bus station I discovered at once that the journey to the island is a regular day out. I'd assumed it would be fairly quiet, but the bus was full and another was filling up beside it. The route to Tsawwassen is across flatlands, rather like the Fens and, like the Fens, there is not much to look at, so I noticed at once when a windmill loomed up ahead on the horizon, very East Anglian. But beside the windmill was a castle. Strange turrets and ramparts pierced the skyline. This was Fantasy Gardens – not to be confused with Fantasyland, which is a very bizarre hotel in Edmonton, Alberta. Fantasyland has theme *bedrooms*, including a pick-up truck. Fantasy Gardens is just a theme park, although it took on an even more fantastic aspect when I learned that the premier of British Columbia, one William Vander Zalm, was living in one of the castles. There was some row going on at the time over whether or not he owned Fantasy Gardens also. If he did, it appeared to have slipped his memory.

Our ferry, the *Queen of Esquimault*, was the size of a cross-channel ro-ro, and loaded to the gunwales with buses, trucks and people. Half of Vancouver seemed to be heading for the island. It was a comfortable journey, but a long one, zigzagging among the islands. At one time we were in American waters, for the border with the United States also zigzags between the islands. Some of these isles were uninhabited, some were big enough to accommodate whole villages. On some there seemed to be only two or three houses. All had pale empty beaches and were clad in fir trees. Off Knapp Island there was a stir of excitement, people swarmed to the side of the ferry, pointing. A few hundred yards away five dolphins leaped in the water. Strangers beamed at each other. There was an air of congratulation aboard. We all felt obscurely flattered that the dolphins should have come out to dance while we were watching.

At Swartz Bay you get back on the coach for the trip down south, through Saanich, to Victoria. I had been told by many people that Victoria is more English than England. The countryside looked fairly English, little towns, farms, villages. After Mt Newton Crossroads large advertisement hoardings began to appear at the roadside. They are known as billboards in North America.

A famous, if sentimental, poem begins:

I think that I shall never see
A poem lovely as a tree.

The American poet Ogden Nash adapted it:

I think that I shall never see
A billboard lovely as a tree.
Indeed, unless the billboards fall
I'll never see a tree at all.

But it was a Canadian, Joni Mitchell, who wrote:

> They cut down all the trees
> And put 'em in a tree museum.
> They charged all the people
> A dollar and a half just to see 'em.
> Don't it always seem to go
> That you don't know what you've got till it's
>   gone?
> They paved Paradise,
> Put up a parking lot.

But things aren't that bad yet on the road to Victoria.

Victoria, like all Canadian towns that are supposed to look like somewhere else, looks like a Canadian town. We all got out at the bus station. Bus stations – I love them. You just can't glamorize a bus station. Round the corner and across the road was the museum, standing in a grove of totem poles. The ones outside, and in Thunderbird Park next door, were painted. The ones inside the museum were weathered down to the wood. Chuck had said that the First Nation people preferred it that way and had resisted early attempts to renovate poles that were disintegrating. They themselves would have allowed them to follow the natural course, ending in a return to the earth, but now they are "Heritage" and must be preserved. I remembered the pink and blue jobs outside the Mohawk Centre in Prince Edward County. And I remembered Bird House City.

Out in the courtyard I sat down to draw a low man on a totem pole. His expression was grievous and he appeared to be in the grip of a large bear, but every time I looked up from the sketch book I found a Tic-tac posing beside him while an obliging husband took a photograph.

"Isn't he *neat*?" squeaked one kittenish two-hundred-pound specimen. It wasn't quite the word I'd have used.

Along the road were the beautiful, imposing Parliament buildings. Opposite stood an equally imposing CPR hotel complete with green roofs, the Empress. At the Empress one can take afternoon tea, as the English are popularly supposed to do. Every other restaurant

Low man on a totem pole – Victoria, Vancouver Island

was offering "English Teas". I went into the Eaton's Centre Mall in search of Canadian coffee. I found it. I also found the Body Shop, W.H. Smith and Marks and Spencer.

I had come all the way to the Pacific Coast and what did I find? Marks and Sparks. I went in, just for the experience of going into Marks on a Sunday, and then sat down in the food hall to drink the coffee and decide whether I ought to go onward, westward, until I stood upon that Pacific Coast and gazed upon the ocean. Shouldn't I do that, after coming so far?

In the end I decided against it. If I was going to be

that picky I ought to have gone the whole hog and begun the journey at the extreme eastern edge of the country, on the Atlantic Coast at St John's, Newfoundland. Anyway, I told myself, I had once seen the Pacific. Admittedly, I was in Australia at the time, but I did know what it looked like. It doesn't look like the Atlantic, for instance, although it is probably as filthy. It is vast, apparently quiet, with seething depths; rather like Canada, come to think of it, but my sea is the North Sea, small, rough and dirty – rather like England, come to think of it. I went back to the bus station.

I realized that I'd been sitting, as it were, on the Canadian side of the bus on the way to Victoria. Going back I saw the English side. Heading towards us was a red double-decker, one of the old London Routemasters. There was a shop called London Shoes, another advertising Oxford sweaters. I also noticed a small eating house called Isobel's Ribs.

Out in the country again we passed a small field, surrounded by trees. Figures moved dimly among clouds of steam and aged stationary engines, boilers and smoke. A banner identified them as the Saanich Historical Artefacts Society. If they are who I think they are, these guys are heroes, industrial archaeologists. While the rest of us sigh nostalgically for the age of steam, they go out to find, rescue and lovingly restore the steam-driven equipment that powered industry and agriculture before the days of electricity and internal combustion. My brother is one of these people. Every so often they break out and have a field day, like this one at Saanich.

The ferry back to Tsawwassen was even more crowded than the one coming out, and loud with Japanese grannies. Asians, that is Chinese and Japanese, outnumbered the rest heavily and, unlike a British crowd coming back from an excursion, were in a terrifically good humour – except for the grannies, who, like grannies the world over, had a lot to say for themselves, none of it good, by the sound of it. The sun was setting and in the distance, all the while, that great American mountain hung magically in the sky.

To save a hike back from the bus station, over the Burrard Bridge and up the hill, I decided to get out of the bus on Cambie Street, put my faith in the grid system, and walk west. Somewhere, I reasoned, I should cross Burrard Street, down near the Jewellery Bazaar and the International Restaurant, and then I should know my way back.

It worked. It was dark by now and the pavements were mainly deserted, although there was plenty of traffic. I did not see one other pedestrian all the way, but there was no feeling of threat, of lurking violence. Later, back in England, I mentioned to a Canadian colleague how safe I'd felt, walking in Canada at night. True, he said, but added that he didn't think he'd want to walk around Vancouver after dark. Still, I know people who won't walk round London after dark. I know people who won't walk in *Oxford* after dark. If I believed everything I read in the local paper, neither should I.

In Montreal, Bill told that once, as he was driving home, late at night, he saw a black family wandering the street and thinking that they might be lost, being out so late, stopped to offer help. The father explained that they were from Detroit. Twice a year, he said, he brought his children to Canada to show them that somewhere in the world it was truly possible to walk the streets in safety after dark.

I heard Detroit mentioned frequently, with a tremor in the voice; Armageddon over the border, the City of Dreadful Night, so close, so menacing, a threat of things as they might be, as they might become.

Archibald Lampman (the Frog Poet of Ottawa) might have been looking into the future when, in 1892, he wrote "The City at the End of Things".

Its roofs and iron towers have grown
None knoweth how high within the night,
But in its murky streets far down
A flaming terrible and bright
Shakes all the stalking shadows there,
Across the walls, across the floors,
And shifts upon the upper air
From out a thousand furnace doors...

And moving at unheard commands,
The abysses and fires between,
Flit figures that with clanking hands
Obey a hideous routine.

Well, he had never seen the production line at General Motors, and neither have I, and probably most Canadians have never seen Detroit, but its spectre haunts them; it is *there*.

* * *

Next morning I went back down the hill, past the Jewellery Bazaar and the International Restaurant, over the Burrard Bridge, on my way to walk again in Stanley Park. At the city end of the bridge precipitous steps lead down to the sands of English Bay, past the imposing façade of the Aquatic Centre. I'd noticed the Aquatic Centre every time I crossed the bridge, and wondered if it might be worth a visit. Could it be an aquarium, a dolphinarium, a maritime museum? It turned out to be the local swimming baths.

On the beach I sat on a log, gazing out across the water. There were logs lying all over the sand. Knowing the Canadian urge to make life pleasant, I wouldn't have been surprised to discover that they had been put there on purpose, especially for sitting on while gazing out across the water, but they might have strayed from log booms coming down from the mountains. I recalled my incredulous astonishment the first time I saw a real live log boom. We had, you must understand, learned about them in Geography.

Out of the corner of my eye I thought I could see a person standing. When I looked round I found that there was indeed someone standing, a great stone figure on a little promontory a couple of hundred metres away. As I walked towards it I thought it had a look of Stonehenge, of ancient monuments: dolmens, menhirs. Close to, it towered above the promontory, a figure built of massive boulders, standing one upon another. It is "Inukshuk", made by Alvin Kanak, an Inuit sculptor of Rankin Inlet, on the western shore of Hudson Bay, and stands looking out over the mouth of this more southerly, warmer inlet, a symbol of hospitality.

"Inukshuk" – Vancouver

While I was admiring Inukshuk I became aware of two figures, evidently engaged in a ritual dance around his feet. Sometimes they faced each other, sometimes they moved side by side, but always their actions were identical. They bent and stretched, leaped, crouched, swung and strutted. Finally they hunkered down and performed synchronized frog hops. It was tempting to think that perhaps they were engaged in some primitive mating rite and I half hoped they might spring simultaneously into the waters of the bay and swim away to spawn in the Pacific, but disappointingly they were just performing aerobic exercises. No wonder they operated as a pair. You'd feel a complete prat doing it on your own.

In Stanley Park, that extraordinary landscape of rain forest and rose garden, the wildlife was pursuing its usual pastime of mugging tourists. I bought a cookie and a coffee from a booth by the lagoon and sat down under a sequoia to eat. Two Canada geese loafed over and proposed sharing the cookie. A squirrel descended from the tree and suggested that I pick out the nuts for him. All three were polite but firm. As we reached the end of the cookie a couple of middle-aged Tic-tacs appeared on an adjacent path. A squirrel sprang out in front of them and ordered them to halt with an imperious paw. When they tried to walk round him a friend arrived to head them off. I looked down and found a third colleague rooting through my shoulder bag. I have seen red and grey squirrels in Canada, and curious tabby hybrids, but the top class of squirrel is black; stout, shiny and expensively upholstered. In Toronto they have sussed that people with cameras would like them to pose, so they do, tails curling with panache, paws in the beseech position. Mind you, they expect to be paid.

I walked back into the city along Robson Street. Last time I was here I was told about Robson Street which is, I was assured, so very European that it is known, German-fashion, as Robsonstrasse.

It didn't look in the least European to me, except in the matter of gift shops, and I wondered why being European strikes people as so desirable. The only incident that reminded me of home was when a lady stopped me in the street and asked if I could give her fifty cents. She was only the third beggar I'd met. The other two were in Montreal.

I was heading for Gastown, where "Gassy Jack" Deighton, a riverboat captain, opened a pub in 1867; that is, he put a plank across two barrels and sold

whiskey to the grateful population of loggers and
gold prospectors. Later a hut was built over the plank.
Things developed rapidly after that. Whether the gas
referred to his liquor or his conversation I don't
know, but Gassy Jack Deighton was more or less the
founding father of Vancouver, and the site where his
saloon first stood is known as Gastown in his honour.
I was looking for his statue which stands at the end
of Water Street, but I never did reach it. What I did
discover was something that appeared to have strayed
from the Saanich Historical Artefacts Society. On the
edge of the pavement in Water Street stands a steam
clock. Steam was escaping from valves and apertures
all over it. A crowd, four deep, surrounded it, waiting
for lift-off, maybe. It clearly did something besides
tell the time, but it was hard to see what.

It was a very long while since I had found a worthy
candidate for the Good Cemetery Guide. I hadn't
seen a decent cemetery since leaving Prince Edward
County, where they are small and rather cosy. I
abandoned the search for Gassy Jack's statue and
turned on to Cordova to begin my final hike through
the city and over the Burrard Bridge. From the
junction with Cambie, I could see what looked like a
war memorial. Perhaps there might be a graveyard in
the area. I started up Cambie, staring with fascination
down side lanes strung with those impenetrable cats'
cradles of overhead wires that knot up every Canadian
city I've seen except, possibly, Calgary. I passed the
Cambie Pub. I'd hardly have noticed it only, as I
approached, I became aware of a dull roaring on the
left, issuing from an open doorway. Inside was a huge

room, dimly lit and crowded with men; just men. I began to take in the fact that there were no women on the street, either, and that all the men, like iron filings to a magnet, were heading in the direction of the pub. Now, I'd been told that pubs, as places to take a quiet and respectable drink with the family, were becoming fashionable, and I'd seen them in Toronto, Montreal, but this place was the spiritual home of Gassy Jack. This was a saloon.

Although the roar was due to the size of the place rather than the level of noise inside, and it all seemed entirely peaceable, I couldn't help thinking of a poem that had been at the back of my mind since Calgary, when I had first discovered the history of Fort Whoop-Up. This poem surely has the world's most memorable first line:

> A bunch of the boys were whooping it up in
>   the Malamute Saloon;
> The kid that handles the music box was hitting
>   a rag-time tune;
> Back of the bar, in a solo game, sat Dangerous
>   Dan McGrew,
> And watching his luck was his light-o'-love, the
>   lady that's known as Lou.
>
> When out of the night, which was fifty below,
>   and into the din and the glare,
> There stumbled a miner, fresh from the creeks,
>   dog-dirty and loaded for bear.
> He looked like a man with a foot in the grave,
>   and scarcely the strength of a louse,

Yet he tilted a poke of dust on the bar, and he
  called for drinks on the house.

The Shooting of Dan McGrew is one of the most
famous ballads by the poet Robert W. Service. It is
often fifty below in Service's poems, where women
are fast and men are hard, by God they are, none
harder than blasphemous Bill MacKie, who died in
the Yukon and was sought out by an old pal who had
sworn to bring him home and bury him decent, with
a gravestone. Old Pal took the coffin along with him
on a Yukon sleigh. The temperature was, on this
occasion, sixty-nine below.

Have you ever stood in an Arctic hut in the
  shadow of the Pole,
With a little coffin six by three and a grief you
  can't control?
Have you ever sat with a frozen corpse that
  looks at you with a grin,
And seems to say: "You may try all day, but
  you'll never jam me in."
I'm not a man of the quitting kind, but I never
  felt so blue
As I sat there gazing at that stiff and studying
  what I'd do.
Then I rose and kicked off the husky dogs that
  were nosing round about,
And I lit a roaring fire in the stove, and I
  started to thaw Bill out.
Well, I thawed and thawed for thirteen days,
  but it didn't seem no good.

His arms and legs stuck out like pegs, as if they
    was made of wood.
Till at last I said: "It ain't no use – he's froze
    too hard to thaw;
He's obstinate and he won't lie straight, so I
    guess I got to – *saw*."
So I sawed off poor Bill's arms and legs, and I
    laid him snug and straight
In the little coffin he'd picked hisself, with the
    dinky silver plate.

Then there were Gum-boot Ben, Windy Ike, Pious
Pete and Sam McGee, who ill-advisedly wandered
north from Tennessee, froze to death and didn't
revive until he was cremated, observing, as he sat up
in the furnace, "Since I left Plumtree down in
Tennessee, it's the first time I've been warm."

Say what you like about Service, he knew what it
meant to be cold. Can't you just see him, skimming
across the snow at ninety below, behind his team, as
the whip cracks, the runners hiss and the Northern
Lights dance overhead?

Yes and no. Service was a bank clerk from Preston,
Lancashire, who took off for Canada at the age of
twenty-one with, by his own account, five dollars in his
pocket. On Vancouver Island he farmed, picking
stones off fields, digging ditches, chopping trees.
When farming palled he went to New Mexico, but in
the end the lure of the bank proved stronger than the
call of the wild. His return to banking saw him head
inexorably towards the Arctic. Every time his
employers moved him he ended up further north,

starting in Victoria, then shifting to Kamloops, BC, then Whitehorse and finally Dawson City, where he took long walks and was inspired to write by reading Rudyard Kipling. He was known as the Canadian Kipling, the Bard of the Yukon, although *The Oxford Companion to Canadian Literature* remarks uncharitably that he can be regarded only as a visiting Englishman. In truth, his time in Canada was only thirteen years (out of eighty) but his *Bar-Room Ballads* and *Rhymes of a Roughneck, Songs of a Sourdough* and *Ballads of a Cheechako*, have been at least as influential in shaping people's idea of Canada as, say, *Rose Marie*.

It was home-time in Vancouver as I took my last walk through the city, and crossed the Burrard Bridge for the last time. The day had a dying fall to it. The sign in the window of the Jewellery Bazaar read CLOSING FOR EVER!

I turned right on to Broadway to buy supper at the Chinese supermarket, and then struck out uphill again on Cypress, alongside the chainlink fence that

The School Cemetery, Cypress Avenue – Vancouver

ran around a school playing-field. And here, when hope was fading, I found what I was looking for. In the corner of the field, right up against the chainlink fence, was a little plot of earth from which rose small mounds, like molehills. Pebbles were laid neatly round each mound, and on each summit grew a plant. They were lettuces. I think that little burying ground on Cypress was my favourite graveyard in all of Canada, where the children had tenderly buried the school guinea-pigs and rabbits and placed their favourite plants on top.

I found it just in time. Next morning I flew back to Toronto.

Chapter Eight

My friend David used to live on the thirteenth floor of a Toronto apartment block that was chiefly memorable for having in the forecourt a fountain made out of enormous Anglepoise lamps. When the charm of the Anglepoise lamps palled he would take off for Goderich, in Huron County, where his family have a cottage on the cliff above the east shore of Lake Huron. It stands in a maple wood, one of a whole string of cottages that sometimes host several generations of the family, assembled for weddings or holidays, sometimes lie empty save for a passing aunt.

The day after I arrived back in Toronto we set out for the cottage. At first road runs south-west, to Kitchener, founded by German settlers and called Berlin – until the First World War. A short detour to the north takes you to Guelph. From Guelph came the man who wrote one of the most famous poems of that war, and drew in it an image that has stayed in people's minds ever since: poppies.

In Flanders fields the poppies blow
Between the crosses, row on row,

That mark our place; and in the sky
The larks, still bravely singing, fly
Scarce heard amid the guns below.

We are the Dead. Short days ago
We lived, felt dawn, saw sunset glow,
Loved and were loved, and now we lie
In Flanders fields.

Take up our quarrel with the foe:
To you from failing hands we throw
The torch; be yours to hold it high.
If ye break faith with us who die
We shall not sleep, though poppies grow
In Flanders fields.

"In Flanders Fields" is not so much admired these days, perhaps because people are better educated about the realities of war and admit that a soldier at the front probably has less of a quarrel with the foe than with the politicians who sent him there in the first place. Even as soon as 1918, only three years after it was written, McCrae's friend Sir Andrew McPhail was writing: "To say that (it) is not the best would involve one in controversy. It did give the expression to a mood which at the time was universal, and will remain as a permanent record when the mood is passed away."

Yet who is more entitled to write about war than a man under fire? McCrae was not a professional soldier but a doctor, and he wrote his poem during the Second Battle of Ypres where he was serving with a

Canadian artillery division. "We saw the show," he said, "from the soup to the coffee." A fellow officer wrote, "John had his dressing station in a hole dug at the foot of the bank. During periods in battle men who were shot actually rolled down the bank into his dressing station."

And "Along from us a few hundred yards was the headquarters of a regiment, and many times during the sixteen days of battle he and I watched them burying their dead whenever there was a lull. Thus the crosses, row on row, grew into a good-sized cemetery."

The poem was written during those lulls, between the arrivals of batches of wounded. In his letters home he did not mention the casualties; no one patient ever stood out in his mind; it must have seemed like a ghastly conveyor belt to him. What worried him most were the animals caught up in the carnage of the trenches; a big Oxford-grey dog ... a little white and black dog with tan spots that sheltered in his dugout ... a wounded horse whose life he managed to save – he always worried about the horses – and his own mount, Bonfire, who went through the war with him and outlived him when he died of pneumonia in 1917, no longer at the front but still working as a doctor behind the lines. His friends reckoned that Bonfire had seen enough active service and instead of returning him to the army for redeployment, spirited him away to quiet, if illicit, retirement.

McCrae would have wanted that. He loved animals. They followed him everywhere, even into his hospital. He was not a great poet, not even a very good poet. The unusual form of "In Flanders Fields" was something he had tried out before, as with the idea of the restless dead. But, just once, he got it right. People liked his poem. The soldiers liked it. Who dares to tell a soldier what kind of poetry he ought to admire?

Lt Colonel John McCrae MD ought not to be confused with another Ontario poet, James MacRae, who, in 1877, mightily objected to corsets.

A shapeless mass, by name a lass,
Is artfully arrayed,
Is neatly bound with metal round
And trimmings wisely made,
And padded o'er with worthless store
To cover unbetrayed
The sad effects, which one detects
When nature is displayed.

After Kitchener the road heads for Stratford, where David's car broke down, a few miles out of town. He had remarked earlier that it didn't like hills anymore. We rode into Stratford behind a pick-up truck that deposited us at the local Honda specialists who hang out in a back street next to an outfit that calls itself Nick and Dan's Collision. I wondered if this could be a theatrical event, some kind of experimental drama; Nick and Dan, endlessly colliding, but it was, of course, another breakdown shop, specializing in shunts and the effects thereof.

We had to hire a car for the rest of the trip, and

stopped to recover with coffee in the park by the river. Stratford doesn't do things by halves. On the highway, at either end of town, is a large sign:

STRATFORD
HOME OF THE
STRATFORD FESTIVAL
AND THE ONTARIO
PORK CONVENTION

Stratford-upon-Avon, England, doesn't have a pork convention, I bet, but apart from that there are similarities. Stratford, Ontario, also stands upon the River Avon, and across the river, from where we were sitting, is the Festival Theatre, where Shakespeare's plays are performed every summer (the next town along the highway is called Shakespeare). In Stratford itself the Bard is everywhere: on Romeo Street, where stands the Romeo Public Water Utility, in the As You Like It Motel, and at the Birnam Wood Arboretum, which is still saplings and is not, at the moment, going anywhere.

Could it be in deference to the Swan of Avon that almost every house has planters on the front steps in the shape of swans?

Canadians don't keep gnomes in the garden, but they have just about everything else, although actual plants can be a bit thin on the ground. Bill and Esther's garden in Montreal is a wilderness of flowers, but that is unusual, although you can instantly spot a Portuguese front garden or a Chinese back garden, intensively cultivated, in Toronto. This may be the result of early English settlers' obsession with lawns; you didn't really feel at home in a colony until you'd got a good lawn going. Unfortunately the Canadian climate is not, on the whole, sympathetic to lawns. Out here in rural Ontario many of the farmhouse gardens are about an acre in size. The house sits in the middle, parallel to the highway. Halfway between the house and the road lie two flower-beds, usually flaunting something hot and red, salvias or geraniums. Everywhere you can hear the buzz of little powered lawn mowers, trimming these miniature prairies.

A garden centre, moreover, doesn't necessarily sell plants, although it sells a great many other things. The doyen of garden centres is Merv's Patio Place at Dublin. Merv's influence can be observed several kilometres either side of Dublin and all the way into Goderich. His concrete sculptures line the highway: rabbits, skunks, raccoons, cattle, horses, squirrels, hen-and-chicks, duck-and-ducklings and, naturally, frogs.

Fashions in garden sculpture change. A couple of years ago the item that appeared most often was a cut-out of a large person, seen from behind and bending down. This you could stick among your petunias and impatiens to give the illusion of someone gardening. No longer, alas. State of the art garden sculpture now is a concrete pedestal on which reposes a large metallic globe, red, blue, silver. I believe this trend has spread north over the border from New York State.

At Merv's Patio Place creatures thronged the

roadside like spectators at a carnival, flanked by globes on pedestals. At a table two of Merv's employees were carrying out field surgery on damaged statues, while on the back lot a few of the superannuated bending figures loitered furtively. David wanted to buy a couple of concrete chickens to go with his hen. He'd kept a whole clutch on the balcony in Toronto, but two had got broken. He confided wistfully that what he would really like is a Holstein. These are the hefty Friesian cattle of the region and their effigies are much favoured by farmers.

Goderich is a lovely town on Lake Huron, built like a square wheel round the hub of Courthouse Square, which is an octagon. It exports salt, which was discovered accidentally in the nineteenth century by a company drilling for oil. The local paper carries news and schedules of the salt boats and grain boats that ply the lake. It is a peaceable place; Wolfe Street runs alongside Montcalm.

Its founder and first citizen was one Tiger Dunlop, whose last will and testament was a best seller and has not been out of print since his death.

I, William Dunlop of Gairbraid in the Township of Colbourne, County and District of Huron, Western Canada, Esquire, being in sound health of body, and my mind just as usual (which my friends who flatter me say is no great shakes at the best of times), do make my last will and testament as follows, revoking of course all former wills.

His bequests veer towards the eccentric, especially in the matter of snuff.

> I leave my silver tankard to the eldest son of old John as the representative of the family. I would have left it to old John himself, but he would melt it down to make temperance medals and that would be sacrilege. However, I leave my big horn snuffbox to him; he can only make temperance horn spoons out of that.
>
> I leave my brother Allen my big silver snuffbox, as I am informed he is rather a decent Christian, with a swag belly and a jolly face.
>
> I leave Parson Chevasse (Maggy's husband) the snuffbox I got from the Sarnia Militia, as a small token of my gratitude for the service he has done the family in taking a sister that no man of taste would have taken.

Goderich also contains a Panopticon. It is the only Panopticon in North America, possibly in the whole world, since the one built at Millbank, London, is no longer standing. It was the invention of the philospher Jeremy Bentham, who wrote, in 1771: "In a panopticon prison ... there ought not to be any where a single foot square, on which man or boy shall be able to plant himself ... under any assurance of not being observed."

The Panopticon in Goderich is the Huron Historic Gaol. It is an octagon, with a lookout tower at the centre, built on the plans laid down by Bentham, thus: " – a proposed form of prison of circular shape having cells built round and fully exposed towards a central 'well' whence the warders could at all times observe the prisoners."

The Huron Historic Gaol is now a kind of penal museum, and no one is confined in it (though they sell you a bail bond instead of a ticket at the door) but on a wall inside hangs an inventory of fines and convictions during the last century. They are, mainly, drunk, drunk and disorderly, just plain disorderly ... and then there is Madame de Montfort, fined two dollars for telling fortunes. I should like to have stood among all those Scottish Presbyterians when Madame de Montfort roared into town.

Round the corner in North Street is the Huron County Pioneer Museum. This was the brain child of Herb Neill, ostensibly a farmer but with a passion for machinery, which he collected, repaired, played with and cannibalized to create new marvels. In his Essex motor he drove around the county collecting artefacts for his museum. Herb was some way ahead of his time in realizing that museum exhibits look far more convincing if they are collected when people have only just stopped using them, instead of being dug up after three hundred years to be reassembled from fragments.

The museum has been enlarged, hugely enlarged, and modernized, but Herb's display of working models still fills several rooms. While the machines go through their motions the air is filled with melody from the Orchestral Regina, possibly the world's largest musical box, being the size of a wardrobe and operated by a drive belt. A brass disc, two feet across, provides the music. However far you stray in the museum, I would guess that you are never out of earshot of the Orchestral Regina, although we turned it off before we moved on to the other exhibits. It plays only one tune.

Beyond the working models, the museum is a treasure house. There are rooms of garments, Indian and Inuit artefacts, a room full of hearses, a whole railway locomotive, utensils, implements ... but what I had come to see was the two-headed calf.

The museum has been so thoroughly modernized that I was at first afraid there would no longer be room for a two-headed calf, once the *pièce de résistance* of any rural museum, but at last I found it ... them ... marvellously, there are *two* two-headed calves in the Huron County Pioneer Museum, not merely two-headed, but two-tailed as well. Strictly speaking, each is made up of two calves, sharing four legs, very realistically stuffed, which is more than can be said of some of the other creatures that share their glass case, animals posed in attitudes that could give taxidermy a bad name and extra point to the ads in the paper reminding you to get your pets innoculated against rabies: slavering bunnies, homicidal raccoons, squirrels from hell.

We dropped in on David's parents for lunch. They have a farm on a hillside, tucked into a loop of the Maitland River. Up near the house are sheep pastures, a pumpkin patch, and a huge barn where live cats, chickens and Steve the ram, who was, disappointingly, out. Out where and doing what I didn't discover. In a hopeful reversal of the usual order of things, David's father has forested the land that was once cultivated; from the edge of the farm down to the river grows mixed woodland: conifers, sweet chestnuts, maples, birches. The twisting river appears at intervals between the trees.

We set out in sunshine to see the trees and under the still-leafy branches did not notice that the sky had darkened. Coming out on the grassy slope below the house we saw that it was going to rain heavily within minutes, possibly seconds, and headed back up the hill. On the way lay a little pool, and as we passed it a little frog leaped from the grass and into the water; a frog; a *live* frog, at last. The first and only live frog I ever saw on that trip. I was so pleased to have found it and, thinking about this later, began to understand why, perhaps, the frog is held in such very tender regard by Canadians – there are no cuckoos in Canada. Long ago, in the days before gas and oil, electricity and central heating, the English awaited the call of the first cuckoo each year as a sign that winter was over, spring begun – or at least imminent. They still do. People still write to the *Times* to record the first cuckoo of spring. In Canada the frog is the sign of spring, the creature that endures through deep cruel winters and sings (not croaks) to herald spring. I wonder if people write to the *Globe and Mail* to record hearing the first frog.

While I was delighting over what was possibly the *last* frog, the storm hit us. Hurricane-force winds roared across-country from the lake. Rain hit the ground like nails, thunder shook the house.

It passed as suddenly as it began, leaving the high hoop of a rainbow in the sky. We hurried back to

Goderich to visit Laithwaite's celebrated cement sculptures at Apple Farm on Highway 8, before another storm came boring over the lake from Michigan. George Laithwaite constructed these unique sculptures mainly during the 1930s, using fieldstone, cement, iron bars, roofing tiles. George could sculpt anything – out of anything. The lion lies down with the lamb; two rutting stags battle for supremacy. One Robert Borden, possibly the prime minister of that name, drives a team of oxen while George himself strolls across the orchard with two buddies, on a fishing trip. The artistic interpretation varies enormously, from the sublime to the God-awful. At the God-awful end are two simpering children on the lawn (they once held up the tennis net) and an extraordinary group featuring two guys stabbing each other while an angel hangs around in the background, either trying to offer assistance or just getting in the way. On the other hand, the stags are magnificent, so is the polar bear and the group of lions, and so, as he looms from a flower-bed, is Moses, framed by a fine stand of walnuts. So imposing is Moses that at first we thought he was God, but an article in the

"Moses" in the bushes
– Goderich, Huron County

local paper said Moses, so he must be. Like the beautiful bird houses of Picton, weather and age and acid rain are destroying George's work. His descendants struggle to keep the sculptures together.

There is no entrance fee; you can just wander in off the highway to admire the show. When the present Mr Laithwaite came out of his farm shop while I was drawing Moses, I thought that he might, reasonably, be on his way to ask me to get the hell out of his front garden, but no, he had just come to offer me a chair to sit on.

We had planned to return to the cottage on the cliff to watch the sunset across the water, but instead another storm came boiling up over the lake; two rival storms, rioting across the sky. Thick greasy clouds seethed overhead while between them the sun set redly and forked lightning ripped the sky on either side of it. Then the rain fell.

After a couple of hours it was still falling but we ventured out to Goderich for dinner. It was a choice between Captain Fats' Fish and Chip shop and the pub. The pub has a restaurant attached to it, but we went for a drink at the bar, first. It was not quite like an English pub – for a start everyone was sitting down – but it was not like the Cambie in Vancouver, either, and a far cry from the Malamute Saloon. Fixed to the door is a brass plate.

ON THIS SPOT
IN 1824
NOTHING HAPPENED

* * *

Goderich was founded in 1827 after which, presumably, things started to happen. According to another notice, inside, this pub is also the Home of the Dancing Security Guard, but if he was there he wasn't dancing.

Back at the cottage, after dinner, we lit the logs in the open fireplace and sat late into the night listening to the storm over the lake. Far out in the dark the light from one ship shone bravely, and through the riot of wind and rain the foghorn called like a woman's voice, a desolate contralto.

Next day it was time to collect the repaired car and return to Toronto. On the way out of Goderich we paused for a visit to the Maitland Cemetery, set among beautiful woodland at the lip of a ravine. On the very edge, above a little precipice, lies the grave of Archibald Lang, first archbishop of the Arctic. He has an igloo on his coat of arms.

At the cemetery gates stands a warning sign, intended for those who wander into the cemetery in search of refreshment.

CEMETERY TAP WATER
NOT
POTABLE
FOR FLOWER WATERING
ONLY

Even Canadian cemeteries have their limitations.

We had one last errand, to collect a pumpkin from the farm to take back to Toronto for Thanksgiving. Unlike American Thanksgiving, which is held in

November and is said to commemorate (although in
fact it doesn't) the landing of the Pilgrim Fathers, the
Canadian version falls in the second week of October
and is the equivalent of our Harvest Festival. As our
Harvest Festival is haunted by marrows, so pumpkins
figure largely at Thanksgiving. Pumpkin pie is a
traditional Thanksgiving dish, and although I knew
that Kathy's pie filling was coming out of a tin, David
and I had plans for the pumpkin.

Chapter Nine

Once known as York – Muddy York – Toronto takes its present name from an Algonquin word meaning meeting place. I had only one day left in Toronto and there were two things I had to see: the Sunnyside Bathing Pavilion and Honest Ed's.

One can go to the Sunnyside Bathing Pavilion, down on the shore of Lake Ontario, to bathe, but on Saturday afternoons it fulfils another function. The entrance is imposing, with a fine flight of steps. People who have just got married go there to have their wedding photographs taken against the steps, the fountains, the colonnade. These are not just any old weddings, either.

The build-up hadn't started yet. David and I had been doing the Thanksgiving shopping for Kathy at St Lawrence Market, and arrived a little early. We strolled up and down, admiring the view. Soon we saw, coming towards us along the wide pavement, four young men in dark morning suits. They advanced in step, unhurried, purposeful, unsmiling; they looked like the Earp brothers and Doc Halliday advancing down the main street of Tombstone for the shoot-out with the Clantons at the OK Corral. They were the advance party. White stretched limos began to pull up, and the rest of the wedding party arrived. The limos were adorned with pompoms. Passing motorists hooted, much as they do in England to express solidarity with striking workers. Three identically dressed bridesmaids in brass lamé, chosen to match, swept along the pavement in impossible heels, like models on a catwalk. The bride arrived. Out of the bushes leaped what appeared to be a small chimpanzee in a morning suit; it was the little brother, too young to go into combat with the Earps. A young man approached, staggering under the weight of an armful of candyfloss. A foot dangled from it. It was either a child or an inflatable bridesmaid.

No sooner had this party dispersed than another took its place. The first lot were Koreans, these were Italians, but apart from the latest set of Identikit bridesmaids, this time in scarlet, it could have been an action replay of the first wedding. By now, white stretched limos were homing in from all directions; some were even cruising the highway until space became vacant. We left. Things were looking dangerous. The prospect of two weddings clashing on the steps was too appalling to contemplate. In the resulting snarl-up of bridesmaids, someone could go off with the wrong husband.

Honest Ed's is on the corner of Bloor and Bathurst. It is a shop, plastered with adverts, one of which sums it all up:

THERE'S NO PLACE ... LIKE THIS PLACE ...
ANY PLACE!

Indeed there isn't. This is the hub of Honest Ed Mirvish's empire; retail, property, theatres – you name it, Honest Ed is into it. Anyone in London calling himself Honest Ed would immediately, and probably rightly, be suspected of being as bent as a nine-pound note. But Honest Ed *is* honest – and great entertainment. The ads begin outside and follow you round.

DON'T JUST STAND THERE – BUY SOMETHING.
HONEST ED'S. *Only the floors are crooked.*

They are, going up and down queasily as Ed's original shop expanded over different properties. The ground floor is given over to household goods, ranging from kitchenware to ornaments. There are utensils made of strange alloys, ornaments that might be on the run from Merv's Patio Place. One corner is devoted to religion, holy statues and a range of titanic rosaries, one seemingly made of small logs; rosaries for smiting the heathen; combat rosaries. Much of the stuff is hideous, but none of it is junk. Those ornaments are built to last.

HONEST ED'S *a fat slob ...*
but his prices keep a slim figure.

The puns become more outrageous.

> HONEST ED'S *an idiot.*
> *His prices are "cents less".*

> HONEST ED'S *a nut –*
> *but look at the "cashew" save.*

On the stairs:

> HONEST ED'S *dangerous! –*
> *because of falling prices.*

Upstairs is what looks like the world's largest jumble sale. Here stand counters heaped with clothes, all new, but cheaper than you would expect to pay second-hand. The basement is a supermarket running a strong line in cheap pet food.

All this began as a modest retail outlet. The rise and rise of Ed Mirvish is a classic success story. His press cuttings are posted outside, in a glass case on the wall of the store. He figures largely in a street mural just around the corner. The next street is known as Mirvish Village, where his son David runs an art book shop. (He also runs the Old Vic theatre in London, saved from ruin when Ed stepped in a few years ago and bought it amid ungrateful growls from the British theatre establishment.) Ed is known to keep rents low for publishers, writers, artists. His own hobby is a little modest ballroom dancing once a week. He is, as the English writer Arnold Bennett once put it, "identified with the great cause of cheering us all up".

Round the back of Honest Ed's I saw some writing

on a wall. STRENGTH THROUGH SOY. It made me sorry I hadn't had time to revisit my absolute all-time favourite graffito, which I once found down near Harbourfront, on a concrete support of the Gardiner Expressway: DWN WTH VWLS.

Driving back to Kathy's we listened to the radio. Alas for Joe and Jacques in Halifax; Parliament was now sitting again or, rather, it was standing up and shouting. The politicians were indulging in that grand old Canadian pastime of filibustering. A fast one had been pulled on the honorable members – by some other honorable members. In the Upper House (the Senate) the Conservative leader had called for a vote on an unpopular measure while all the Liberals were out of the Chamber, on the dubious grounds that there is nothing in the Constitution to say that you cannot do this. The Liberals were currently seeking their revenge. Broadcasters are not allowed into Parliamentary sittings, so the journalists were lurking by the doors and shoving in a microphone every time they were opened. Shocking scenes were gleefully broadcast. Venerable old gentlemen of seventy-five, who had sat in Parliament since the 1930s, had been up all night climbing on their desks, banging their shoes on the table, commandeering the Speaker's microphone and reading passages from the Old Testament and *Hamlet*. Since all this was equivalent to a riot in the House of Lords, I was sorry not to be watching it on television.

We returned to scenes of catastrophe. Kathy's oven had broken down, stranding her with the monstrous Thanksgiving turkey, only slightly cooked. Everything else was still entirely raw. *Impasse*. The turkey would not fit into David's modest oven, but, much worse, it was a non-kosher turkey in a predominantly kosher neighbourhood. According to Jewish dietary laws (which are strict) meat dishes and milk dishes may not be prepared in the same pans, and meat must be killed in an approved manner. No one with a meticulously-kept kosher kitchen was going to admit Kathy's goyische turkey from the supermarket.

We leaped into the car, with the pallid fowl upon my knee in its tin, and drove to Kathy's parents to keep the beast warm while Kathy went in search of an electrician, with wan hope, for as well as being Saturday it was the Jewish Sabbath.

We drove home and Kathy took off again, this time returning with Johnny, an affable Armenian Jew, discovered conversing with a Chinese neighbour in fluent Cantonese. Not only was he a linguist, he was an electrician, and repaired the oven in ten minutes flat, Kathy departed to retrieve the turkey and I went out on to the back step with a sharp knife and the pumpkin we had brought from Goderich. We had chosen it with great care. It wasn't one of your regular round pumpkins; it was long, wider at one end than the other. I was going to carve a pumpkin lantern for Thanksgiving dinner, but not just any old pumpkin lantern. This was going to be fashioned in the likeness of Moses, the Moses of Goderich, in honour of George Laithwaite. It was a pretty good likeness, though I say it myself. When David arrived we applied ourselves to the problem of installing a candle in Moses, which was difficult on account of his shape. Eventually we bored a hole through the bottom and rammed the candle into it; a breakthrough in pumpkin technology.

It was after the dinner that I finally got to speak to the person who had once seen the Great Frog of Fredericton. Apparently the frog, although just a regular tadpole when young, had been fed daily on bran mash by its doting owner, and when fully grown was the size of a dog.

When I flew home the following evening, I watched the lights of Toronto fall away below the Boeing's wing and thought of the Great Frog. It had never been far from my mind since I first heard of it, three weeks ago in Halifax; my first Canadian frog. It seemed a fitting symbol of that peacefully barmy stratum that runs under the topsoil of Canada and cannot be seen from a distance. Would that, could that, survive the breakup of the nation, if and when it came? And I thought too of Joni Mitchell:

Don't it always seem to go
That you don't know what you've got
    till it's gone?